CRUNCH

BY

KEVIN ALLEN

Photography by Bruce Bennett Studios

TRIUMPH
B O O K S

CHICAGO

CRUNCH

Printed in the United States of America

This book is available in quantity at special discounts for your group or organization. For more information, contact:
Triumph Books
601 South LaSalle Street
Suite 500
Chicago, Illinois 60605
(312) 939-3330
Fax (312) 663-3557

Book design by Sue Knopf
Jacket design by Salvatore Concialdi

ISBN 1-57243-303-5

To my buddy Larry O'Connor, for the wondrous
hockey overload years in the 1970s, when it didn't
seem the least bit unreasonable to drive three hundred
miles on a Friday night to watch Gordie Howe play a
World Hockey Association game.

Contents

Foreword

BY JOHN FERGUSON

"Fighting has been a part of hockey for fifty years.
It will be with us another fifty years. Count on it."
—John Ferguson, after he retired from the NHL in 1972

I got my start in the National Hockey League after the Montreal Canadiens had lost four straight to the Chicago Blackhawks in the 1962-63 season. They were manhandled physically. It did help that I had made the All-Star team in the American Hockey League with the Cleveland Barons and led the league in penalty minutes. In my first game, "Toe" Blake put me on a forward line with Jean Beliveau and Bernie "Boom Boom" Geoffrion, and I responded physically twelve seconds into the game. The fight with Ted Green was my first time dropping the gloves. I also added two goals against Eddie Johnson and an assist in a 4-4 tie.

Toe Blake also told me that both players needed protection and I put it into my mind that I wanted to be the meanest son of a bitch on the ice in every game thereafter.

The game of hockey earned its form of intimidation from the warriors of the trade: the Bauns, the Hortons, Reg Fleming, Ted Green (who once had a bounty on his head), Ted Harris, Orland Kurtenbach, Forbes Kennedy, Garry Howatt, Stan Jonathan, Chris Nilan, Tiger Williams, Behn Wilson, Nick Fotiu, Paul Holmgren, Dave "The

Hammer" Schultz, Wayne Cashman, Dave Brown, Willi Plett, Clark Gillies, Glen Cochrane, Bob Plager, and Terry O'Reilly. The present-day tough players, who are hard to play against, include: Kelly Chase, Tony Twist, Stu Grimson, Jim McKenzie, Matt Johnson, Marty McSorley, Tie Domi, Darren McCarty, Gino Odjick, Brent Myhres, Ken Baumgartner, and Joe Kocur.

One of the best fights I ever witnessed was when two mountains collided in the forms of Clark Gillies and Willi Plett in the Nassau Coliseum on Long Island, New York. It was a classic punch-out.

I remember being behind the bench coaching the New York Rangers in the Philadelphia Spectrum when Paul Holmgren and Nick Fotiu ran up the hallway behind the players' bench and continued their battle between the fronts of the players' dressing rooms. There were sparks flying off the cement from their skate blades. The next time we played there they had iron bars between the two rooms.

We all find our hands vulnerable. I had a fight with Ed Westfall, then of the Boston Bruins; he put his skate up during the scrap and I punched through it. My thumb was hanging by some skin. I had an operation in Boston right after the game to save my thumb, missed eighteen games, and came back and finished the year with a steel cast.

Another year I punched the ice and broke a knuckle after Wayne Maki ducked my punch. I never missed a game, but I had to freeze the hand before every game and put it in a bucket of ice every period.

One of the big fight draws of our time was when Tie Domi and Bob Probert, then of the New York Rangers and the Detroit Red Wings, had a rematch at Madison Square Garden. *USA TODAY* had the tale of the tape on the front page of the sports section.

Violence in today's National Hockey League is more in the form of high-sticking, cross-checking from behind, and a drawing of blood from high sticks than the old form of good toe-to-toe fighting between two heavyweights. The Stanley Cup playoffs have been void of fighting lately, and the institution of the two-referee system will curb some of the scraps. The influx of many European players into the National Hockey League will certainly make it tough for a willing combatant to find a fighting partner. But Canadian junior hockey still produces the best battlers, and fighting is still a large part of the entertainment value in the NHL. Michael Peca is probably the best open-ice hitter today, but he never picks his spats. Bryan Marchment may use his knee on occasion, but when he hits his opponents straight up, he puts the fear of God into them. Despite the controversy over violence, nothing will ever be able to take the big hit out of the game.

Terry O'Reilly was a hard-nosed winger who became captain of the Boston Bruins because of his never-quit style of play. The Bruins rewarded him with the home team's penalty box when they closed the Boston Garden. And if anyone can find the visiting team's penalty box, which the Bruins gave me, there is a huge reward for finding it.

If I missed anyone, they are on the honorable mention list. May you all continue to crunch.

The famed picture of Bob Probert with the mouse under his eye is appropriate for one of the most intimidating players in NHL history. Despite a career undermined by a battle with substance abuse, Bob Probert in his heyday was a feared, effective competitor. He even was named to play in the NHL All-Star game in 1998. That was the season he scored 29 goals while leading the league with 398 penalty minutes. With 209 PIMs in 1998-99, he now ranks fourth on the NHL's all-time list with 3,253.

Introduction
WARRIOR CODE

The National Hockey League only dates back to 1917, but its honor code shares ideals with the Roman Empire.

This is not to suggest that Julius Caesar ever contemplated playing the neutral-zone trap against the Britons, Gauls, or Belgic peoples. But the soldiers of the Roman Legion were committed to a level of performance that seemed almost superhuman to adversaries. They were undaunted by pain or hardship, unwavering in their allegiance to the cause, and unbelievably loyal to the pre-battle pledge of "coming back with their shield, or on it."

So it is with players who wear NHL sweaters. Although hockey's gladiators may not risk being carried away from a game mortally wounded on a shield, there is a tradition of fierceness and acceptance of pain in the sport that is almost unfathomable to outsiders. An honor code exists in hockey that makes it unseemly to complain about injuries, dishonorable to shrink from physical contact, and unacceptable to miss a playoff game except under extreme circumstances.

Sometimes broken bones don't even constitute extreme circumstances.

The tradition of physical toughness is as important to hockey as power-play goals and Hall of Fame goalkeepers. To call hockey a contact sport is a disservice. Hockey is a nuclear sport, explosive and awesome in its ability to inflict pain and injury upon its participants. Skaters reach speeds of up to thirty miles per hour. Pucks travel as fast as one hundred miles per hour. Twenty skaters move off and on the rink every forty-five seconds. Players occasionally brandish wooden, aluminum, and graphite sticks like they are medieval maces. All of this takes place on an ice surface that is only about sixty-five yards long and twenty-six yards wide. Violent collisions aren't just likely in hockey; they are inevitable.

This contained environment helped create a special breed of athlete, whose adherence to hockey's special warrior code has led to an exaggerated expectation that players can overcome almost any injury in order to play. This play-at-all-costs tradition seems to have been passed down silently from generation to generation. There is no need to say anything when you have witnessed Philadelphia Flyers center Dave Poulin don a flak jacket to play with broken ribs, or seen Edmonton Oilers defenseman Kevin Lowe play with one of the many injuries that punctuated his long, impressive career. Young players studied hockey's warrior code under masters of the craft. Adam Graves watched Mark Messier play through pain and discomfort in Edmonton, and Mike Keane learned from Bob Gainey's perseverance in Montreal. Scott Stevens honed his toughness with Rod Langway as his mentor. It is a hockey tribal ritual that is an essential part of the fabric of the game.

Current NHL players know the story about how Toronto Maple Leafs defenseman Bobby Baun scored the game-winning overtime goal on a fractured fibula in Game 6 of the 1964 Stanley Cup Final. They know that he refused to have the leg X-rayed after the game, and that he hid from team doctors until showing up minutes before Game 7. He played nearly thirty minutes in Game 7, freezing his leg every few minutes to make the pain more bearable.

They have heard the tale of how Maurice "Rocket" Richard was knocked unconscious during a Game 7 in the Stanley Cup semifinals

Ron Hextall (right) gets tangled up with New York Rangers tough guy Darren Langdon. Hextall has earned a reputation as one of the most aggressive goaltenders in NHL history. He protects his crease area by any means necessary.

in 1952 and came back to score the game-winner. After a bodycheck by Boston's Leo Labine, Richard fell and hit his head on the knee of Boston's Bill Quackenbush, which knocked him unconscious. With four minutes left in the third period, Richard returned to the game, took the puck, and went the length of the rink with it to beat Boston goalie Jim Henry for the winning goal. Later, Richard told teammates he didn't pass the puck because his vision was too blurred to pick them out.

They know that Mario Lemieux played in the 1991 Stanley Cup finals with back pain so severe he couldn't bend over to lace his own skates, and that he scored a goal a few hours after he completed radiation therapy for Hodgkin's disease.

It's difficult for a hockey player to ask for a day off to nurse a minor wound when he knows that Hall of Fame goaltender Glenn Hall once played 502 consecutive complete games—from October 6, 1955, to November 8, 1963—without a mask.

Given that historical precedent, it's no wonder that players often don't opt for Novocain when they are stitched up between periods, and that the vast majority of NHL players believe it is their duty to return to the game immediately after their wounds are closed. This is a sport that comes close to embracing zero tolerance for "soft players." There seems to be no room in the NHL fraternity for players who won't play the game as if it is combat.

General managers, coaches, and players worship those among them who can deliver a big, jarring, open-ice hip check that sends the victim pinwheeling through the air like a gymnast in the midst of a badly-blown dismount. The same general managers, coaches, and players have even more respect for the victim who gets up from that wallop, checks the number of his assailant for future reference, and goes about his business as if he is immune to the pain. Those who believe hockey is simply about goal scoring aren't watching the game closely enough. Hockey is about intimidation, bravado, endurance, toughness, and the pain tolerance that creates those goals.

This is a sport in which some of the most revered players are those who explore the outside edges of the rulebook. This is a sport in which an elbow thrown in the face of an opponent can be both a penalty and a respected play. This is a sport in which scouts talk about needing to find prospects who have the proper "mean streak." This is a sport in which coaches lament their shorthanded teams and yet regularly beseech their general managers to bring in more players with higher penalty-minute totals.

A pro hockey coach may woo the goal scorer, but the tough, rugged, heavy hitter is his true love. Coaches have had a century-long admiration for the player who will do whatever is necessary. Since hockey's beginnings in the late nineteenth century, there have been many players who have sensed the crucial moment when flattening an opponent with a devastating bodycheck could change the momentum of a game. Coaches can recite long lists of defeats transformed into victories due to one player's willingness to use his body to break his opponents' bodies or spirits.

Hockey is frequently an artistic sport in which players glide gracefully over the ice and connect on precision passing plays that seem to have been designed months before by a skilled choreographer. But hockey is more often a cruel sport, a primal sport, a sport in which the difference between winning and losing may come down to the ability to execute in the face of human suffering. Hockey's artists usually garner most of the attention, their exploits trumpeted each night on the national sports shows. This book is a salute to those who toil and sweat, who often go unnoticed beyond their own kind.

This book is about hockey's legion of warriors, the players who pledge to come back from every game with their shield, or on it.

CHAPTER ONE

A Stitch in Time

PLAYING WITH PAIN

Hockey parlance labels it as "playoff makeup." Stitches. Welts. Mouses under the eye. Black-and-blue bruises. Yellowed wounds. Purplish face discoloration. Not the kind of stuff that comes from Maybelline.

They are the badges of honor earned in a sport in which the most exalted athletes are those who can tolerate the most physical discomfort in pursuit of the Stanley Cup. No other sport, not even football, pays such homage to the notion of playing in pain. It's a minimum requirement for those wanting to be accepted into the fraternity of top NHL players. In the old days, a player like former Montreal Canadiens winger John Ferguson would insist that a player could overcome any injury with "a little tape and aspirin."

When Ferguson was a general manager of the New York Rangers, he would jokingly send a message to his players that he expected them to make a Herculean effort to stay on the ice, just as he had done when he was playing in Montreal. "Your knee is bad?" he would ask. "That's a long way from your heart."

"The code among our hockey athletes is if you have a pulse, you play," says Vancouver Canucks general manager Brian Burke. "There is no logical explanation for their pain threshold."

Supporting this notion is a long list of players who impress their teammates with an iron will in the face of snapped bones and deep gashes. Everyone in the league has several stories about what players have endured in order to stay off the disabled list. These tales are retold regularly to give the tradition more legs as it travels through time. Exaggeration isn't even required to add luster. When it comes to injuries, the truth is sometimes even more gruesome than anything that can be conjured up in one's imagination.

"I remember Ron Greschner almost having his ear severed in half," says former NHL goaltender John Davidson. "He needed about eighty stitches to close it up, but he was back out there playing in the third period."

In today's NHL, medical care is far more sophisticated, and team physicians have at least put a stop to players coming back to play too soon after they suffer concussions. Players simply aren't allowed to compete if playing will exacerbate their injuries. Salaries and stakes are too high to risk long-term injury for the sake of one game. Today's physician will allow NHL players to maintain their tradition of playing with pain, but not at the expense of their long-term well-being. This probably wasn't as true in the 1970s and before, when players were even more warrior-like in their preparation.

Davidson had both of his knees replaced on September 1, 1998. In the back of his mind he wonders if there is some connection to the level of abuse his body suffered from 1973-74 to 1982-83. He recalls rushing back too soon after one particular knee surgery. "I had a three-inch cut on the inside of my left knee for cartilage work," Davidson says. "Two and a half weeks later I was playing a game in the American League to come back. I took the gear off at the end of the game and I had blood running down my leg. True story. I hadn't even healed. That's the way it was. They were always trying to get you back playing."

In former New York Rangers goaltender John Davidson's day, goaltenders were often hurt more in practice than they were in games. Davidson remembers that during the regular season he would have bruises tattooed all over his body. Today, some teams even employ practice goaltenders to prevent wear and tear on the first-string netminder. Although goaltenders are still susceptible to injuries, they are protected more by today's equipment.

St. Louis Blues vice president Ron Caron remembers from his days with Montreal in the 1970s that even the team doctor had difficulty keeping players out of the lineup. During the Canadiens' run for one of their four Stanley Cups, Dr. D. G. Kinnear ruled that Rejean Houle and Doug Risebrough shouldn't play because of injuries. Caron says coach Scotty Bowman requested a second opinion from another doctor outside of Montreal.

"He must have treated them with a special instrument they didn't have in Montreal because—guess what—they were able to play," Caron says, laughing. "Scotty Bowman knew those two had a lot of guts and could play through anything."

Montreal players took pride in staying in the lineup. Caron was walking through the dressing room after one game and saw Bob Gainey take off his skate to reveal an ankle twice its normal size. "I remember saying, that isn't right, you had better get that X-rayed," Caron says. "But he played in the next game and then had it X-rayed. When he came back it was in a cast and he was gone for three weeks. But he played two games on it."

Broken toes. Shoulder separations. Cracked ribs. Sprained ankles. These are merely a few of the injuries that NHL players will play with, especially during the playoffs. Sportswriters are reluctant to speculate on whether an injured player will be able to perform in the postseason because players regularly defy odds. Teammates weren't completely surprised in the 1995-96 playoffs against Detroit when St. Louis Blues goaltender Grant Fuhr put on a knee brace and contemplated trying to play with a torn anterior cruciate ligament. He couldn't do it, but just the fact that he tried showed the kind of moxie NHL players boast when it comes to injuries.

"Hockey has that gladiator mentality," New Jersey Devils defenseman Ken Daneyko says. "That's why it is such a great game.

Guys play through anything. A guy has to be awfully hurt to miss the playoffs."

Going into the 1998-99 season, Montreal winger Mark Recchi was the NHL's reigning Iron Man with 543 consecutive games played. His streak ended at 570 games on December 12, 1998, when he missed a game due to pneumonia. He hadn't missed a regular-season game since March 31, 1991, when he was in Pittsburgh's lineup. He was still years away from matching Doug Jarvis's league record of 964 consecutive games played or Andy Hebonton's 630 consecutive games for the New York Rangers and Boston Bruins from 1956 to 1964. Cal Ripken's streak of consecutive baseball games played is incredible, but given the physical nature of hockey, the iron man tendencies of hockey players are equally impressive. After all, no one is slashing Ripken's wrists and trying to erase him with a hip check while he is running the bases or devouring a grounder at third base.

"If you can put on your skate, you'll play in our sport," Recchi says. "Guys tend to suck it up a lot in the playoffs. Sometimes I don't know if we're stupid."

Not at all, according to Pittsburgh Penguins team physician Charles Burke. He insists there is nothing barbaric or reckless about the NHL players' tradition of playing through pain because, in today's game, modern testing gives team physicians an accurate assessment of injuries. Nobody is allowed to play with a concussion or a compound fracture, and a situation like Baun hiding from the doctor wouldn't occur in today's game. He says today's players also know more about their anatomy than players of the past. They train so rigorously that they have come to understand their bodies' limits almost as well as the physician understands them.

"We work with these players all season, and they trust us," Dr. Burke says. "The players know what's going on. Some of them have

Mario Lemieux (kneeling) is treated by Pittsburgh trainer Skip Thayer. Lemieux, always a major target for abuse, played with pain throughout his NHL career.

had the injuries before. Nobody is going to risk their careers. We have a clear understanding of all of the factors."

That said, Dr. Burke says there is no exaggeration to the players' tradition of playing with pain. Through the years, he has watched several Penguins endure much pain to stay in the lineup, none more than Mario Lemieux. He overcame two major back surgeries, Hodgkin's disease, and an assortment of minor injuries to score 613 goals in 745 regular-season games and 70 goals in 89 postseason games. Many top NHL scorers are spared from much physical abuse because they are sleek and, hence, difficult to line up for a big hit. At 6-foot-4, 225 pounds, Lemieux was such a large target that he was subjected to more than his fair share of big hits in his career. "People don't realize how much (back) pain Mario Lemieux was in when he played," Dr. Burke says. "It was debilitating. He couldn't tie his shoes, but he would go out and score three goals."

This willingness to play with pain is as much a part of playoff hockey tradition as overtime and the seven-game series. During Game 3 of the 1964 Stanley Cup semifinals, Hall of Famer Terry Sawchuk, in traction for a pinched nerve in his shoulder, checked himself out of a hospital because he wanted to play for Detroit, whose Red Wings were trailing. In 1978, Toronto's Lanny McDonald, playing with a football face mask to protect a broken jaw, scored an overtime goal to beat the New York Islanders in a Game 7. NHL vice president Jim Gregory, a former Toronto general manager, remembers marveling at Bobby Orr's bravado in playing through his numerous knee injuries. "The Leafs doctor told me his knee was so bad one year that he couldn't believe he was playing," Gregory remembers.

The assumption today is that players in bygone years probably "got the needle" far more often to deaden the pain of serious injuries.

"In those days that's what you were supposed to do," says former NHL defenseman Bob Plager, now a pro scout with the St. Louis Blues.

Plager admits that he can hardly walk as a result of the abuse he received during his career. "I got one leg twice the size of the other, and my shoulders are still sore," he says honestly. "But I would do it again. Yes, I would do it again. But I wouldn't blame today's players if they didn't want to do it—there's so much money, and so much at stake."

Hall of Famer Dave Keon, a member of the Toronto squad, told former NHL coach Harry Neale that he will never forget seeing Red Kelly play on a severely injured knee to help the Maple Leafs win a Stanley Cup.

"Keon told me after they won he was in the dressing room, and he looked in the shower room and saw that Tim Horton had Kelly in his arms and was carrying him out of the shower," Neale says. "The freezing had come out of his knee. Now the game was over, and Kelly was in agony. Keon said it made him cry."

Plager says players in his era were ordered to play without anyone actually saying the words. "They brought out the needles in the playoffs. Twenty-three needles in your arm so you could play, and then after the game you cried," Plager says. "We always thought we were lucky to play the game, and today's players think we are lucky to have them."

These stories help fuel players' determination to stay in the lineup in the postseason. "When you are young you learn that's how it is done. It filters down," says Boston Bruins winger Dave Andreychuk. "You see other veterans do it. When I was in Buffalo, Mike Ramsey played with a broken hand in 1983, and Gilbert Perreault came back from a broken thumb in 1985. And it's really not just in the playoffs. It's all year long. You just hear about it more in the playoffs."

Ken Danyeko would have taken off a few games had he broken two fingers in the regular season. But when it happened in the 1994 playoffs, he ordered a special cast made, cut his gloves to accommodate the cast, and suited up for the next game. What makes the

NHL playoff warrior mentality more impressive is that players are playing highly intensive games almost every other day for two months. Coaches insist on the probability that no team has ever won the Stanley Cup without having a handful of players overcoming injuries to stay in the lineup. For example, Brendan Shanahan played through a herniated disc to help the Red Wings win a Stanley Cup in 1998. Shanahan wasn't nearly the player he would have been healthy, but he refused to sit out, knowing that even at half-speed he could still make a contribution.

"People would be amazed if they knew how banged up players were during the playoffs," says Detroit Red Wings associate coach Dave Lewis. "Sergei Fedorov played with broken ribs when we won the Cup in 1997. Some players couldn't put on the gear between games, but they would be out there playing at game time."

Montreal Canadiens assistant coach Dave King says very few players "take the parachute" when it comes time to overcome pain to stay on the ice. Is it peer pressure that keeps players performing after their faces are sewn back together? "A little bit," Andreychuk says. "You've seen older guys do it, and it puts pressure on the younger guys to do it."

Those who don't play through aches and pains do stick out like the sore thumb they won't play with. "Everyone has a different makeup," Daneyko says diplomatically. "Some guys have a better pain tolerance and some heal quicker than others, but certain players are being known as softer than others and some are known to play through anything."

Chicago Blackhawks center Doug Gilmour owns the latter reputation. He couldn't walk because of a foot injury during the 1994 playoffs but managed twenty-eight points in eighteen games. He had surgery right after the season.

"No one has ever criticized hockey players for being soft," says Boston's Ken Baumgartner, who was Gilmour's teammate at the time. "People would probably be amazed to see what players go through just to make sure that they are available for the game. Doug Gilmour had (torn ligaments) in his foot that required it to be frozen every time he put on his skates. There are certain players you have to tie down to keep them off the ice surface, no matter what the injury is."

Gilmour could barely walk with that injury, but he played on it, and he played effectively. Montreal coaches were impressed with Mark Recchi's willingness to keep his streak alive, particularly late in the 1997-98 season when he played on a badly swollen foot. "It's one thing for a guy to play to fill a uniform," says Montreal assistant coach King. "When [Recchi] plays, he performs."

Players are rather matter-of-fact about playing with pain. It's no big deal, they insist. That's part of the bravado that is a staple of hockey. "With a broken foot—after the first week or so it's mended," says Florida Panthers forward Alex Hicks. "It's just dealing with the pain. You can freeze it and play, so that's what guys do."

Tomas Sandstrom was another NHL player who seemed to be able to ignore pain to stay active in the playoffs. Kings defenseman Rob Blake remembers witnessing Sandstrom suffer a cracked bone on the side of his leg as a result of a rugged hit by Edmonton defenseman Craig Muni. "A week later he was out skating, ready to play again. He was one of the best at getting ready to play again after an injury," Blake says.

It's difficult to know how much players endure because it's also common practice to hide injuries, particularly in the playoffs. Players don't like opponents to know they are hurt, especially if they have a slight shoulder separation or a bad bruise that can be exploited with a slash or a heavy check. When a player is listed as having a

In the 1999 playoffs, Phoenix center Jeremy Roenick, shown here hauling down Eric Lindros, came back from a shattered jaw to play weeks before anyone thought he would be ready.

groin pull it's usually NHL-speak for "we don't want to tell you." It's called a groin injury because there is no way an opponent can exploit a groin injury.

Most players prefer to suffer in silence, but sometimes their heroics are front and center. Phoenix Coyotes center Jeremy Roenick earned his badge of courage in his first NHL playoff season while playing for the Chicago Blackhawks against the St. Louis Blues. He took a high stick to the mouth, and immediately went to the referee instead of the bench. He wanted to give his team a five-minute power play more than he wanted to seek medical attention. His legend as a warrior began a few minutes later when he scored the winning goal on the power play.

"Jeremy came to the bench, and (he still) had his tooth in his mouth," says Darren Pang, who was playing for the Blackhawks then. "His face was all cut up and the tooth was on his tongue. The guy got a five-minute major and Jeremy scored the winning goal on the ensuing power play. That's playoff hockey. That's where you get your name in this sport. That's why players like that get paid more money."

It's more than just tradition that keeps players in the lineup. Sometimes coaches like injured players in the lineup for inspiration as much as for production. "Even if they can't play effectively, they will probably be reliable defensively, and they will provide leadership on the bench," Brian Burke says.

But sometimes the reason why stars will play with pain is far more basic. "Gordie Howe with two broken ribs," Jim Gregory says, "is still going to be better than the 21st player on your roster."

One of the best illustrations of playing through pain and injuries occurred in the 1999 Stanley Cup Final, when a badly-injured Brett Hull became the Dallas Stars' hero in their Stanley Cup-clinching, 2-1 Game 6 triple-overtime win against the Buffalo Sabres.

"When the dust settles, Brett Hull is going to be an incredible story," Dallas coach Ken Hitchcock says. "What this man did to go on the ice and what we had to do between periods to get him back on the ice was incredible."

Hull played with both of his groin muscles shot and a torn medial collateral knee ligament. Between periods, he had to have his injured areas numbed and he had to receive heat treatment, ice treatment, and tape. "I really don't think I could have played a Game 7," Hull admits.

Hull scored at 14:51 in the third overtime period (at about 1:30 A.M. Sunday morning) to end the second-longest Stanley Cup final game. On the replay, Hull can be seen almost limping toward the front of the net to bang in his own rebound against Dominik Hasek. The goal was controversial because Hull's left skate was in the crease before he scored, but not even the Sabres would deny the Herculean effort Hull made to score in that situation.

Hull's only grimace came after the game, when he was told that Hitchcock had compared his performance to Bobby Baun's effort in 1964. "I'm no Bobby Baun—that's for sure," Hull said. No player wants to infringe upon the Baun legend—one of the greatest mind-over-pain performances in professional sports history.

BOBBY BAUN

When the bone in Bobby Baun's fibula snapped in the third period of Game 6 of the 1964 Stanley Cup Final, he recalls that it sounded "as if a cannon had gone off."

Yet the Toronto Maple Leafs defenseman insists that he didn't know his fibula was fractured. Perhaps it would be more accurate to suggest that Baun simply didn't want medical confirmation of the fracture. Carried off the ice in considerable pain, he remembers telling the doctor in the Detroit Olympia infirmary that he wanted "to get it taped up just to see if I can go." It was the league championship series, and his only real thought was that he wanted to get back on the ice in time to face the Detroit Red Wings in overtime. The Maple Leafs trailed 3-2 in the best-of-seven series, and the season would be over if they lost this game.

Toronto coach Punch Imlach didn't even know Baun had returned to the bench early in overtime. "He called for Carl Brewer and (Kent) Douglas to go out, but I told Kent I was going, and that's when I went in and took the shot from the blue line," Baun remembers.

Imlach was quoted in the newspapers the following morning, saying Baun "was so charged up and raring to go that he just leaped over the boards."

With his injury frozen by Novocain, Baun jumped into the play and found himself with the puck at Detroit's blue line. Baun, then twenty-seven, says he took his "home-run swing" at the puck, but the shot was fluttering like a knuckleball from the moment he made contact. The puck struck Detroit defenseman Bill Gadsby's stick and danced over goaltender Terry Sawchuk to give the Maple Leafs a 4-3 victory and force a Game 7. More importantly, it created the legend of the NHL player who scored with a fractured leg.

What makes the story more attractive is that Baun wasn't a goal scorer by even the most liberal of definitions. He had scored two goals in sixty playoff games before finding the net behind Sawchuk, and he never scored another playoff goal after scoring the famous goal. When he retired in 1972-73, Baun still had only three playoff goals in ninety-six playoff games.

Baun originally hurt his leg when he was struck by Gordie Howe's shot. But he didn't hear the snap until the next face-off when he spun around to keep Howe from roaring toward the net. Players in that era weren't surprised when they heard Baun played on the fractured bone. Although Baun stood 5-foot-8 and carried 180 pounds, he was known as a rugged, intimidating defenseman. He was a devastating bodychecker, quite capable and willing to slam opponents along the boards.

What's usually forgotten is that Baun's shot tied the series 3-3, and that he came back to play Game 7 on the broken bone. When Baun was able to play on the damaged leg in the overtime of Game 6, everyone assumed he had a severe bruise. To prevent medical scrutiny of the injury, Baun hid out at a friend's farm for the two days between games. He refused to have the leg X-rayed.

"They couldn't find me," Baun says. "I kept my leg in an ice bucket for almost forty-eight hours. I arrived at the Garden at 6:45 and had them tape it up and freeze it."

Given the tradition of the times, it seems logical to conclude that the Maple Leafs weren't in a hurry to find Baun and drag him to the X-ray machine. They needed Baun. Carl Brewer was playing on a leg injury that had to be frozen for every game in the Stanley Cup Final. Red Kelly was playing on a badly injured knee, courtesy of a double-check by Howe and Bill Gadsby in Game 6. When the series was over, he would enter the hospital in a wheelchair.

Baun had only played a few minutes to score the goal in Game 6. He played about twenty-eight minutes for the Maple Leafs in their 4-0 triumph in Game 7, mostly in excruciating pain. "Game 7 was a real problem. The freezing wouldn't stay," he says. "They were freezing it every ten minutes."

After the game, Baun still didn't join Kelly at the hospital, according to wire reports at the time. He didn't go to the hospital until the next day, when X-rays revealed a hairline fracture of his fibula. To this day, he's not sure how he was able to play Game 7. "It was mostly mind over matter," Baun says. "Doctors have told me I had a high pain tolerance."

Baun wasn't the first NHL player to play in the Stanley Cup Final on a broken bone. Three years before, Detroit's Marcel Pronovost had played in the championship series with a cracked ankle. *The Windsor Star* reported Pronovost performed "gallantly, but not effi- ciently." That's what gave Baun's legacy a long shelf life—he mixed a high level of efficiency with his valor.

CHAPTER TWO

Set for a Collision Course

BODYCHECKING

The message that the New Jersey Devils sent to the Detroit Red Wings in Game 2 of the 1995 Stanley Cup Final was essentially delivered by a truck.

At 6-foot-2, 225 pounds, defenseman Scott Stevens is one of hockey's big rigs. He's a diesel on skates, option-filled with durable construction and a wide range of powerful gears. One can imagine the fleeting moment of terror that must have filled schoolboy-sized Detroit Red Wings winger Slava Kozlov the instant he realized Stevens had locked onto him for a monstrous hit in the neutral zone. Kozlov, who had scored a goal earlier in the game, was streaking across the ice like a Ferrari on the Autobahn when Stevens hit him head-on. In the stands, gawkers stood to look, as if they were witnesses to a highway wreck.

As Kozlov was crumpling, the Devils' momentum swelled.

Although watching the game from three thousand miles away, Los Angeles Kings defenseman Rob Blake, one of the league's top bodycheckers, said he could feel how Stevens's wallop had changed the complexion of the game.

"It's one of the hits I will always remember," Blake says. "A hit of that caliber, which doesn't come very often, can definitely change the momentum of the game."

New Jersey Devils defenseman Scott Stevens, right, jousts with Detroit Red Wings power winger Martin Lapointe during a clash in front of goaltender Martin Brodeur. Stevens, whose playing style is a salute to strength, toughness, and experience, is one of the league's most effective checkers.

In this case, it could have changed the momentum of the entire series. The Devils won Game 1 in Detroit, but were trailing 2-1 in Game 2 when Stevens found Kozlov in violation of the hockey commandment that stipulates *Thou shalt not move east and west in the middle of the ice with your head down.* Just to put an exclamation point on the hit, Stevens skated past the Detroit bench and started to point at every Red Wing, suggesting they all would be next on his hit list. An analysis of the Devils' 1995 Stanley Cup championship run generally centers on Martin Brodeur's goaltending, or Claude

Milt Schmidt, shown here in 1946 falling over Bill Moe, was a physical player as well as the Boston Bruins' top offensive player. In the 1940s and into the 1950s, a team's top players, such as Detroit's Gordie Howe and Montreal's Maurice "Rocket" Richard, were expected to also be the team's toughest players. "They had to score all of the goals and win all of their fights," says former NHL player Max McNab.

Lemieux's Conn Smythe Trophy performance, or even defenseman Scott Niedermayer's coast-to-coast goal-scoring rush in Game 2. However, those around the league know that Stevens's hit on Kozlov was one of those moments that define a series.

Since hockey's origin, the big, booming hit has been one of its most valuable weapons. The size of players may have changed, but Sprague Cleghorn was probably smacking opponents with as much intensity in the 1920s as Eddie Shore was in the 1930s, or Leo Boivin in the 1950s, or Bobby Baun in the 1960s, or Stevens and Blake in the 1990s. Through the years, players have used big hits to intimidate, erase, and instill self-doubt in opponents. Even in this era, when

New Jersey's Bobby Holik demonstrates one way of spilling an opponent onto the ice.

all the players spend time in the weight room, size is a weapon that's still used effectively.

"Once you make players aware that players who come across the middle have to keep their head up, so they don't think they have enough time to do what they want, then you have succeeded in what you are trying to do," Blake says.

Seeing a teammate waylaid, as the Red Wings did when Kozlov was down, can deflate players. "After that hit," Blake says, "you just know that everyone on the bench said, 'You have to watch coming across the middle, he's ready to get you.' Everyone on that bench knows that the ice isn't as open as it was two minutes before a hit. Momentum can change that much."

As this picture shows, there's always plenty of action behind the net. Those caught with their head down during the scramble for the puck pay the price, as did this member of the New York Rangers.

Dallas coach Ken Hitchcock has witnessed that situation from both sides. He's seen his team's morale rocket after 6-foot-5 defenseman Derian Hatcher crushes an opposing forward. He's also coached teams on which players were demoralized by hits against their teammates. "It just changes things dramatically. It can have a huge effect," Hitchcock says. "When you have a team on their heels and they are taken advantage of physically, they aren't the same team."

The reasons why coaches admire the big hitters aren't all that complicated. Here's what a hitter may be able to accomplish by catching an opponent with his head down:

Menacing New York Rangers defenseman Jeff Beukeboom leaves his feet to smack Philadelphia's John LeClair in an effort to take him out of a play. Leaving your feet to make a hit usually earns a boarding penalty.

Sending a Message

NHL players spend hours in the weight room building up their bodies, but few know how to prepare themselves mentally for the key moments in a game. A big hit usually does more psychological than physical damage. When a big hitter decks an opponent, it's the hockey equivalent of the "slap in the face" challenge. Through the years, some teams have become unglued by this—they either shrink from the physical challenge or become so incensed by the hit that they play out of control. Either way, the big hitter has changed the complexion of the game.

Willi Plett was a highly underrated fighter in his day. His punch seemed as explosive as a jackhammer. "He was the only man I saw who actually scared (Bob) Gassoff," says Bill Clement, a former Philadelphia teammate.

Players look to establish a cadence with a hit, to set the drum beat for their march to victory. One of the best examples of this occurred in the 1990 Western Conference Final, when Mark Messier launched a one-man assault against the Chicago Blackhawks in Game 4 at Chicago Stadium. Messier decked several players and cut a couple with his stick to lead the Edmonton Oilers to a 4-2 win. The prevailing wisdom is that Messier's wickedly wonderful performance in that game was the key to the Oilers' Stanley Cup championship. "He should have gotten four years in prison for that night," Madison Square television analyst John Davidson says tongue-in-cheek.

Detroit general manager Ken Holland says the importance of the big hit often depends on who is being hit. "A big hit to me is like a big save," he insists. "If a goalie stops a great scoring chance, it gives your team a lift. If it's a big limited guy hitting a big limited guy, it might not mean much. If it's a big defenseman laying out a skilled player, that's definitely a message."

Terminate Without Prejudice

In the early years, this was as barbaric as it sounds. Players probably would have felt no remorse about trying to injure another player to knock him out of the game. Sprague Cleghorn's own team once suspended him for playing too viciously in a playoff series. Knowing Boston's Derek Sanderson had a bad knee, Montreal player John Ferguson targeted him during one playoff series. He erased him from the series with a hit on the knee behind the net.

In this era, when players are more unified by the players' association, there is far less talk about intent to injure. But there is plenty of discussion about intent to intimidate. Players seem to know which players can be rendered ineffective with constant banging.

"You can still eliminate a guy with a big hit," says Vancouver general manager Brian Burke. "Some guys, if you get them with a big pancake hit, they disappear for the rest of the game."

Former defenseman Bob Plager recalls then-St. Louis coach Scotty Bowman ordering him and defense partner Noel Picard to lay some licks on Philadelphia's Andre Lacroix in their playoff series in 1968-69. Lacroix was one of Philadelphia's top scorers that season with 56 points in 72 games, but he was only 5-foot-8, 175 pounds. "Scotty said he didn't want him to have a shot on goal," Plager remembers. "So in the first period, we had the two wingers circle back and I

John LeClair gets decked by an Ottawa defenseman in front of the net. Most forwards accept the notion that they will be knocked down if they set up in front of the goaltender. Part of a defenseman's job is to clear traffic in front of the net.

hit him, and then when he got up, Noel hit him again. It wasn't the greatest check, or even the hardest check."

But it must have been hard enough, because Lacroix didn't get a point in the series.

Although opponents may not be looking to injure star players, occasionally they do. In 1998, the Dallas Stars finished No. 1 overall in the regular season, but premium scorer Joe Nieuwendyk was injured by a tough hit along the boards by Bryan Marchment in a playoff series against San Jose. Marchment caught Nieuwendyk in a vulnerable position close to the boards, and rode him into the boards. Nieuwendyk suffered a knee injury. The Stars beat San Jose in that series, but had difficulty scoring thereafter and eventually lost to the Red Wings in the Western Conference Final.

Creating Turnovers

The purest reason for the big hit is to create turnovers. The idea is to level the player, erase him from the play, create chaos in the offensive zone, and pounce on the loose puck. Former NHL coach Harry Neale says one of those plays by Colin Campbell helped lift his Vancouver team years ago in a playoff series against Calgary. Campbell nailed Willi Plett with a clean, hard wallop. "We scored on the turnover, and it really picked us up," Neale remembers. "We needed some early success, and Colin must have been salivating when he saw Plett coming."

In today's hockey, defensive pressure is an offensive weapon.

"Physical play plays a huge role in forechecking," says Dallas coach Ken Hitchcock. "The hard-checking physical player is always a significant player in your group. When you put real pressure on someone with physical play, it can have a huge impact on how they perform."

Acts of Retribution

Big hits are often just a means to settle the score, to show the opposing team that you won't be intimidated.

In days gone by, teams could respond to a big hit by sending out the tough guy to exact some revenge. With the instigator penalty now providing the fight-starter with an extra two minutes, that isn't always the best way to go. But sometimes it's necessary to match big hits. "You know if you hit a star player, you have to watch your back," Rob Blake says.

Crowd Adjustment

A big hit can help a home team get its bench and crowd fired up and into the game. Conversely, an away team can silence a home crowd by walloping one of the home players.

Plager remembers in the 1960s when his late brother Barclay would try to catch "The Golden Jet," as Bobby Hull was known, getting ready to take off through the neutral zone. Barclay would lay out Hull with a textbook hip check. "It would really bump up our bench," Bob Plager remembers.

All of these factors play a role in a big hit, but none are foremost in the mind of the player making the hit. The best hitters are those who instinctually know when it's the right time to step up, just like a pure goal scorer seems to know when a scoring chance is about to occur.

"The funny thing about hits is that it's very similar to getting yourself in scoring position," Blake says. "So much is anticipation—it's knowing where the puck is going to go and where the player is going to get the puck. You have to catch him by surprise. Now in our league, if a guy is ready for you to hit him, it won't be a big hit."

New York Islanders defenseman Denis Potvin, wearing the "C," was skilled as a bodychecker as well as on the power play.

The exploding glass on this check is an illustration of how rough it really gets along the NHL boards. Players take note of which opponents are timid about playing along the wall or in the corners.

On the one hand, modern-day players' increased size and strength makes them better prepared to face big hits. On the other hand, the increased size and strength raises the potential for calamity.

"Hitting techniques aren't any better than they were years ago," says Vancouver general manager Brian Burke. "With the kids getting bigger and stronger, it's no longer like an automobile collision. It's like two freight cars colliding."

With hockey's offensive style of the 1980s and early 1990s giving way to a tight-checking defensive game, Colorado's Joe Sakic says players are subjected to more abuse each season. "I'm hit a lot more now than I was when I first came into the league [in 1989-90]," says Sakic.

Today's game plans are now designed with heavy hitting in mind. In the 1970s and before, shifts of top players could be a minute to one minute and thirty seconds. Today, even top players are asked to keep their shifts to thirty or forty seconds. Coaches don't want players pacing themselves to last longer or passing up a check because they are tired at the end of a lengthy shift.

"We want everyone to play with tremendous energy all over the ice," Hitchcock says. "I think the game now is much more physical than it was fifteen years ago."

Some might argue with that contention. Television analyst John Davidson, whose NHL career started in 1973, remembers that what players may have lacked in size a quarter of a century ago they made up for with pure aggressiveness. He remembers solid players like Doug Jarrett (Chicago Blackhawks and New York Rangers, 1964-77), who were able to have a significant impact on the game because they knew how to hit.

"When the pass was going across the ice diagonally, he would turn his body and throw it up in the air at you," Davidson says. "One game he hit (Detroit's) Bill Hogaboam so hard I thought he was dead."

New Jersey defenseman Scott Stevens sends New York Rangers player Paul Broten for a tumble along the boards.

Hall of Famer Denis Potvin (New York Islanders, 1973-88) was another player whose ferociousness is sometimes underrated. "He didn't have real long legs, but he had a wide body," Davidson remembers. "If you admired your pass or shot, the next thing you knew you were doing a cartwheel into the third row. He could be vicious."

The size of today's smashers certainly makes a major difference. When Stevens or Blake connect, it's like having a bundle of bricks fall on your head. Stevens has been an intimidating presence since he signed his first NHL contract with the Washington Capitals in 1982. Even well into his thirties, Stevens is considered one of the league's top hitters.

"With a lot of guys, you look to light a fire under them," says David Poile, who was a general manager in Washington when Stevens was drafted. "With Scott, we wanted to calm him down a little bit."

Stevens's aggressiveness got the better of him in his early years. Opponents preyed upon his temper's short fuse. Even though coaches continually told him how important it was for him to stay on the ice and out of the penalty box, it didn't take much to goad him into fighting. Even though tough guy Dave Brown played just a few minutes a game for Philadelphia, and Stevens was a crucial member of Washington's defense, Brown was masterful at getting Stevens to drop his gloves.

"We wanted him to play under more control, but we were happy to have Scott the way he was rather than try to instill that in someone," Poile says. "It was never any fun to play against Washington with Scott in the lineup. He wanted a piece of every guy who came down the ice against him. He played hard every night. Still does."

Over time, Stevens learned to pick his spots for fights. But he has never surrendered his role as an intimidating bodychecker. Stevens's place as one of hockey history's top hitters is summed up best by Poile's rhetorical question: "What fun is it for some forward to dump it into Scott's corner?"

Stevens's coach at the time was Bryan Murray, now Florida's general manager. Murray had many talks with the young Stevens about skating the fine line between aggressiveness and recklessness on the ice. Stevens used to hurt the Capitals by getting saddled with misconducts.

"Now he is one of the league's most conscientious players," Murray says. "And over his career he has been one of the most consistent physical players. What made him so good is that he learned to get a piece of everyone, even if they put a great move on him. He went after big guys, little guys. He didn't care. He was a great fighter, too, and fought the heavyweights even when we didn't want him to."

Stevens is a stand-up hitter who simply runs over his opponents. He punishes opponents, but most players are far more terrified of the low hit that threatens their knees. Most NHL players consider those who come in low dirty players. "There is a fine line," Blake says. "It's probably four or five inches—you go too low, it will hurt too many players. These players are almost out of control, putting out anything to hit you. If you watch Scott Stevens, he uses his full body. He's not sticking out his leg to catch you."

With the average NHL salary now more than $1 million per season, players are talking more about cheap hits than they have in the past. "There's definitely a code about how to hit," Blake says.

Blake effectively uses his derriere as a checking weapon. Former Kings teammate Doug Zmolek, who now plays for the Blackhawks, calls the move Blake's "ass cruncher." He begins skating backwards, allows his opponent to move wide against him, and then he backs into them along the boards with nuclear force. "Guys have joked about it with me," Blake says. "They see it coming, but they get locked in and can't seem to get out of the way."

He began using that method after suffering severe shoulder injuries. "That's where I have the most padding on my body," Blake says.

Heavy hitters like San Jose's Bryan Marchment and Pittsburgh's Darius Kasparaitis don't get the same respect as Stevens and Blake because players complain they hit "dirty." Former players who watch Marchment and Kasparaitis say they are simply playing the same way that everyone played in the 1950s and 1960s.

"I would love those guys on my team," Plager says. "When the Blues play Marchment now, they worry about him. They say 'Watch that Marchment, keep your head up.' Now we have the whole team looking out for one guy. He's already helped his team just by being dressed and being out there. Kasparaitis is the same way. You worry about him and it takes away from your game."

Darius Kasparaitis, one of the NHL's most intimidating hitters, is shown here jockeying for position with New York Islanders forward Todd Bertuzzi.

NHL Director of Officiating Bryan Lewis has also noted that today's players react differently than the players of yesteryear. "Acceptability has changed," Lewis concedes. "Players all make up their own minds about whether the hit was legal or not."

It's always said that NHL players in the 1950s and 1960s kept their sticks down. But this photo of Toronto's Ed Shack (No. 23) trying to ride Boston's Guy Gendron behind the net would suggest that wasn't always the case.

Television has helped fuel that attitude, says John Ferguson. "There is so much television involvement that every extraordinary slash is so visible to the public," he says. "In the old days, you never saw it."

Today, replays run from every conceivable angle, and sooner, rather than later, players decide they were walloped outside the rules of the game. The stick was too high, or the knee was out, or they were in a vulnerable position. Former players didn't have any video aids to help them judge how hard they had been hit, or if they had been wronged.

Plager and his brother were among the league's best hitters when they played. "I watch now and players are mad when they get hit. If I was playing today, someone would be attacking me all of the time. Today's players don't think you should do it," he says.

Former players had no reservations about trying to knock an opponent into the third row or beyond. Plager hit Eddie Shack so hard that both swear he did two full revolutions in the air. Shack's own stick cut him as he was rotating above the ice. According to the legend, the doctors sewed up Shack and told him he was fit for duty.

"Hell, no," Shack said. "I'm staying right here because those Plager boys are still on the ice."

John Ferguson was another player who could run over a player at high speed. "I hit Ulf Sterner so hard one night in New York that it knocked him right back to Sweden," Ferguson says. Sterner's NHL career lasted four games. Ferguson didn't think much about Sterner after that until he was in an elevator in Stockholm, Sweden, and a woman identified herself as Sterner's wife. "She said, 'You hit my husband and ruined his NHL career,'" Ferguson says. "I actually did hit him pretty hard."

Hall of Famer Tim Horton was also a hard hitter, and older players say Brian Glennie delivered his share of stingers in the 1970s. But one of the best all-time hitters was Leo Boivin (1951-52 to 1969-70). He nailed many players with his open-ice hits during his playing days, and a couple more after he became a coach. Boivin could never forget his bodychecking instincts, particularly when he was coaching in St. Louis.

"Leo would get involved in practice sessions during our breakout drills," Plager remembers. "He would stand at the blue line and knock people down. He would have a little grin. 'Keep your head up. That's how you get hurt, son.'"

Players in the 1940s, 1950s, and 1960s seemed to use the hip check much more than today's players, particularly on the open ice. Rob Blake theorizes that this has to do with the fact that the pace of the game wasn't as fast years ago, when it was easier to zero in on your target. Brian Burke believes that hockey has become so con-

Boston Bruins winger Sergei Samsonov is smashed to the ice by New Jersey defenseman Scott Niedermayer during a goalmouth scramble.

servative in defensive planning that youngsters are scared out of trying open-ice hits. "We teach our kids that (passing up) scoring chances is a terrible thing," Burke says. "And when you miss a hit like that, you are giving up a scoring chance."

In today's game, when power play goals are frequently the difference between winning and losing, Ken Hitchcock won't do anything to discourage heavy hitting, even if it occasionally leads to excess penalties.

"As a coach, I don't think you want to plant second thoughts in your players," he says. "You want them to initiate, not hesitate. You don't want them to go out and think all of the time. They will start to freeze. All you want is that there be an action penalty rather than a reaction penalty."

Burke thinks there's a difference between hitting today and the hitting of yesteryear, because there is a difference in the way the

The hip check is becoming a lost art in the NHL. It was far more popular in the 1960s. St. Louis Blues' Phil Roberto could testify to that, based on the tumble he took on a hip check in a 1968 game.

game is played now. Hits in the past generally led to scoring chances, and scorers cashed in those chances.

"You don't see the fortunes of the game change as a result of a big hit, because it's just so hard to score in our league," Burke says. "You might see less result, but not because the hit is less valuable."

Teams and players learn from a big hit. Kozlov proved something to his teammates when he came back to play in the game after Stevens had short-circuited his senses. He insisted on trying to play, even though some teammates told him not to. "After that series we knew we had to get bigger and stronger," says Detroit general manager Ken Holland. The Red Wings brought in Brendan Shanahan and Joe Kocur, and gave Lapointe and McCarty more prominent roles.

As important as a big hit can be, John Davidson still believes that a hit's significance depends on the circumstances. Take the Stevens hit on Kozlov, for example. "If the Kozlov hit would have come in 1998, instead of 1995, would that have had a big effect on the Red Wings? Not at all," Davidson says. "Back then they were still learning how to win. If you threw a big hit at Kevin Lowe in the 1980s, would that have affected the Edmonton Oilers? No, it wouldn't. The effect of a hit sometimes has as much to do with circumstances as anything else."

THE HIT ON BOBBY ORR

One of the most memorable hits in NHL history occured on April 2, 1969, when Toronto Maple Leafs defenseman Pat Quinn knocked out Bobby Orr with an open-ice smack.

During Game 1 of the Bruins-Maple Leafs playoff series in Boston Garden, Quinn caught Orr with his head down just as he was embarking on one of his famous charges up the ice. There was an audible thud when they collided. The media reported the check was clean, but referee John Ashley called a five-minute penalty for elbowing. Given the mood of the crowd, the five-minute major assessment may have prevented a riot.

As it was, fans went after Quinn, pelting him in the penalty box with debris. One fan even hit Quinn in the head with his fist. Quinn was happy to see a policeman come over until he realized the Boston cop was also an Orr-lover.

It didn't help that Quinn and Orr had gotten into a fight a few weeks before. *The Toronto Star* reported Quinn's account of the fight: "He hit me one good shot on the head when I was down. But I hit a good one when we were standing up and split his lip. It's not a decent fight unless you take at least one good punch."

Boston fans didn't appreciate anyone messing with Bobby, which explains why they began chanting, "Get Quinn, Get Quinn," after Bobby was helped off the ice, suffering from whiplash and a concussion.

Now the coach of the Toronto Maple Leafs, Quinn still insists the hit was clean. He views it as one of the most memorable moments of his career because it was difficult to catch the speedy Orr in open ice. It was also memorable because of the crowd's reaction. "I'm proud I survived that night," he says.

CHAPTER THREE

Hit Me with Your Best Shot

SHOTBLOCKING

The international border between courage and lunacy is located precisely at the point when a National Hockey League defenseman sprawls to block a slap shot.

Shotblockers are among the NHL's bravest competitors. They essentially risk their well-being each time they drop to the ice to block a shot before it gets to the goalkeeper. Consider that St. Louis Blues defenseman Al MacInnis has a radar-gun-proven, one-hundred-mile-per-hour slap shot, and that many of the league's top shooters have been clocked in the mid- to high-90s.

Although hockey players appear to be like Robocops to the average fan, their protective covering isn't as extensive as it seems. They are vulnerable at the ankle, upper leg, back of the leg, torso, and, of course, the facial area. This may be why the shotblocker is an endangered species in the NHL. Fewer players are blocking shots these days than were blocking them in the 1950s, 1960s, and 1970s.

"Blocking shots is the most courageous thing to do in hockey—to lay your body on the line and know your sole reason for doing it is to let the puck hit you," says Detroit Red Wings associate coach Dave Lewis, a former shotblocker.

Nothing illustrates the raw danger of the practice more than the experience of St. Louis defenseman Chris Pronger in the 1997-98 NHL playoffs. He suffered heart arrhythmia—an irregular heart rate—after

Phoenix center Bob Corkum shows the proper technique for blocking a shot without sprawling along the ice. The most experienced shotblockers can drop in front of a shot with perfect timing to ensure that mostly their shin pads are in the line of fire.

he was struck in the chest by a slap shot from Detroit defenseman Dmitri Mironov. Pronger doubled over with the puck cradled in his equipment. When the referee's whistle stopped play, Pronger stood up and skated a couple of strides before collapsing.

"His eyes were wide open, and rolled up and off to the side," says Detroit winger Brendan Shanahan. "He looked frozen. To the players, we knew something was wrong."

Pronger's heart rate returned to normal when he was admitted to the hospital, and subsequent tests revealed no lasting heart problems. It was deemed to be an isolated cardiac problem caused by the trauma to the chest, but doctors admitted it was possible that Pronger's heart may have stopped briefly, although they couldn't be sure.

Having seen what can happen, how can players continually throw themselves in front of those heavy drives from the point? Tradition is the simple answer. Since most of these players were kids, they have seen veteran players give up their bodies in the name of winning.

The sport lost one of its top shotblocking craftsmen when Mike Ramsey retired in 1996-97. If Ramsey wasn't the best shotblocker in the 1990s, he was certainly among the top contenders for the title.

Red Wings coach Scotty Bowman put Ramsey in a class with Al Arbour, Rod Langway, Ulf Samuelsson, and Bob Goldham as the best shotblockers he has seen. "Goldham was like another goalie back there," Bowman says. "And what makes Arbour so interesting was he wore glasses when he did it."

Ramsey paid a price for blocking shots. He fractured his nose, lost six teeth, and felt his helmet split twice. When he lost the teeth, he was hooked as he was going down, and his head was spun into the shot. All of his shotblocking exacted a toll. When Ramsey retired at age thirty-five, he said he was doing so because his body was telling him it had known enough pain.

When former teammates remember Ramsey, they will picture him sitting in front of his dressing stall with his body attired in ice bags. "He epitomizes the nonrecognized athletes who have the dirty jobs to do," says Dave Lewis.

Experience is considered the most important element in shot-blocking. Ramsey began blocking shots when he joined the Buffalo Sabres after helping USA win the gold medal at the 1980 Olympics.

"I grew up playing with a tennis ball in the park," Ramsey says. "Everybody jumps in front of it there, and that's where I learned it— the angles, the timing."

It's a big leap from stopping tennis balls to jumping in front of laser shots from the blue line. Yet veterans such as the Stars' Guy Carbonneau and Detroit's Steve Yzerman continue to drop in front of shots. The Red Wings center considers shotblocking "an art form." He says when a shotblocker has the right timing on his sprawl, "it's like executing the perfect dive."

One problem today: the dangers are greater. The vast majority of NHL players can fire the puck with lethal velocity.

Today's shotblockers learned their technique from veteran players. The art is passed down from generation to generation. "If you know how to do it, you should never get hurt," says former St. Louis player Bob Plager, who never thought twice about blocking a shot during his career. He watched Arbour block a countless number of shots without a scratch—OK, without a serious injury. "I saw him get cut," Plager says. "I saw him get his glasses pushed into his face, but nothing major."

Dave Lewis blocked his share of shots as a NHL defenseman in the 1970s and 1980s, and he improved by watching Bert Marshall block shots for the New York Islanders. "His body was just beat up from getting hit by pucks," Lewis remembers.

Former NHL goaltender John Davidson marvels at shotblockers young and old. His former New York Rangers teammate Carol Vadnais (1966-67 to 1982-83) was among the best he saw, particularly in the postseason. "He might do a flamingo (raising one leg) and let a shot get past him in the regular season," Davidson says. "But in the playoffs he would stop a shot with his face."

Courageous or not, there is still no clear-cut consensus on whether shotblocking is as important as it was years ago. The puck is moving

The art of shotblocking, demonstrated here, demands that the artiste have the courage, timing, and ability to abandon the self-preservation instinct.

so quickly now that some goaltenders believe shotblockers actually do more harm than good because they occasionally obstruct the goaltenders' vision. If the blocker misses the shot, it's difficult for the goalie to pick up the puck as it emerges from under the shotblocker's body.

Secondly, players' increased quickness has set up the shotblocker to look silly sometimes. Coaches wince when they see their penalty killer go down to block a shot, and the point man pulling back the puck and skating around him—creating an instant five-on-three advantage for as long as it takes the defender to get back on his feet and rejoin the play.

"Twenty years ago, players were more deliberate in their shots," Lewis says. "Now, as soon as you go down, you are setting yourself up to get beat. But if you know how to do it, it's a great tool."

Ramsey believes that some players will always have a feel for it. "It's a matter of timing and knowing the shooters," he says. "It's not something you teach. You don't go to hockey school and learn how to block shots." By studying shooters' tendencies, a potential shotblocker can avoid embarrassment. Patience and quickness are equally important to a shotblocker, according to Ramsey.

"You know whether some guys are more inclined to fake or not," Ramsey says. "You know, if it's (Wayne) Gretzky or Adam Oates, if you go down, they will probably dish off. Sometimes you just have to wait them out."

Then there is the issue of whether it's all that wise for multi-million-dollar athletes to be risking broken bones to continue a practice that seems more rooted in tradition than sound defensive logic.

Players do get hurt. San Jose defenseman Bob Rouse broke a bone above his eye blocking a shot for Detroit in a playoff series.

CRAIG LUDWIG

Defenseman Craig Ludwig would have no reason to feel like an old fossil if not for the fact that his old Dallas Stars dressing room stall was once a museum.

More than one teammate or member of the media stopped by to view the shinpads that have protected Ludwig's legs since the 1970s. He received them from trainer Dave Cameron when he was a college freshman at North Dakota, and has been wearing them ever since. When Ludwig played in the 1999 Stanley Cup Final, his pads were older than twenty-one-year-old teammate Jon Sim.

"They were old when I got them," Ludwig says. "When you are a rookie like I was, you don't get the new stuff."

Ludwig keeps the pads in working order with improvised repairs and a healthy dose of duct tape.

"I just don't like new equipment," he shrugs. "I see guys now that go through five pairs of skates in one season. I've had the same pair of skates for three years."

Equipment guys have all but begged him to put on some new skates, but Ludwig won't budge. During the Stanley Cup playoffs in 1999, he estimated that his skates

"Rouse is not typically a shotblocker," Ramsey says. "And those things can happen."

The shotblockers' credo is simple: The ability to get up is more important than the ability to go down.

had only two more weeks before they disintegrated. "They are about to fall off of me," he says, laughing.

Although a large number of hockey players are superstitious, superstition plays no role in Ludwig's love of vintage equipment. "It is a comfort thing," he says.

What makes the ragged nature of his pads even more remarkable is that he's one of the league's premier shotblockers, meaning he's constantly trying to throw his pads toward a shot coming at him at speeds greater than eighty-five miles per hour. His well-being depends on the duct tape.

His shinpads are so legendary in the sport that the Hockey Hall of Fame has requested he donate them for display after he retires.

"I got two letters saying they wanted to put them in the Hall," Ludwig says. "I said, 'No thanks, if you take them, you have to take me,' and I never got a letter again."

Ludwig's plan is to display the pads in his bar in Wausau, Wisconsin. Most likely he will attach them to the wall with duct tape.

CHAPTER FOUR

Linebackers on Skates

POWER FORWARDS

Nouveau hockey fans who believe the power forward concept was introduced in the 1980s with Clark Gillies, or in the 1990s with Cam Neely, Eric Lindros, or Keith Tkachuk, have never looked closely enough at Gordie Howe's rap sheet.

Howe defined the role of the power forward even before the hockey world knew how important a power forward could be. He was a naturally muscular, 6-foot, 205-pound skilled forward who came to the NHL in 1946-47 when many of the top players still weighed 165 pounds. Howe had the skill to be a scoring champion, the size and strength to dominate most of the players in the league, and enough competitiveness and nastiness in his heart to strike fear into everyone.

Harry Neale, one of Howe's former coaches, remembers how Gordie left scores of wounded in his wake in 1977-78 when he tenaciously led the New England Whalers to the World Hockey Association Championship series. Howe's leap from the NHL to the WHA helped improve the credibility of the maverick league, but Howe didn't just cash checks and coast. He ferociously led the Whalers in goals and scoring, and was among the team leaders in penalty minutes.

"He was a miserable guy to play against," Neale remembers. "He had no conscience when he hit you with his stick. Players didn't touch him very often."

Gordie Howe (right), considered one of the top power forwards in NHL history, scores in this 1952 game against the Boston Bruins. In the foreground is Hall of Famer Ted Lindsay (No. 7).

That was the season Howe turned fifty years old. He was nine years older than his coach.

When the Whalers met the Edmonton Oilers in Game 1 of the playoffs that season, Neale spied Edmonton's young defenseman Dave Langevin cross-checking Howe in the back several times in front of the Oilers' net. Neale was friendly with Langevin, and thought it his duty to warn Langevin that Howe wouldn't take that kind of behavior for very long before he'd launch an attack without warning. Neale remembers the conversation went like this:

Neale: "I'm not saying you should let him score, but if I was you I would just tie him up. Don't cross check him."

Langevin: "Screw off, Harry, what's the old bastard going to do? He's fifty years old."

Neale: "I'm telling you, just tie him up, don't cross check him."

In the next game, Howe drove to the net again and Langevin followed after him. Before he could begin his assault on Howe's back, Howe unveiled his plan.

"Just as Langevin starts, Gordie came over the shoulder with his stick, with his blade turned, and hit Langevin and cut him," Neale says.

It wasn't as if Langevin hadn't been warned.

Most general managers probably would argue that an All-Star goaltender is the most coveted player in hockey today, and a top defenseman is a close second. But the elite power forward—a big, strong player who can be both an intimidating presence and an offensive producer—may be the rarest player in hockey. Every year around the National Hockey League trade deadline St. Louis Blues general manager Larry Pleau finds himself amused by the media analysis of each team's pressing needs.

"I laugh when they say a team is looking for a power forward," Pleau says. "There are so few of them around, and every team is looking for them. And those who do have them don't give them up."

The Hockey News has provided some quantitative evidence to support the contention that power players are in short supply. Each year the publication, reputed to be the bible of hockey coverage, bestows the High IQ honor on NHL players who are judged to be among the game's elite power forwards. The "IQ," an acronym for "Intimidation Quotient," is determined by multiplying the player's goal total by three and adding his amended penalty minute total, minus misconducts. To qualify for High IQ status, a player has to have at least thirty goals and one hundred amended penalty minutes.

In 1997-98, Keith Tkachuk, Pat Verbeek, and Eric Lindros were the only three players to earn the High IQ badge, which illustrates the uniqueness of this type of player. However, the broader definition of a power forward covers a wider range of players. Veterans like Carolina Hurricanes' Gary Roberts, Tampa Bay Lightning's Chris Gratton, Edmonton Oilers' Bill Guerin, New Jersey Devils' Jason Arnott and Detroit Red Wings' Brendan Shanahan, Martin Lapointe, and Darren McCarty clearly meet the requirements to be power forwards on most general managers' lists.

"To me, a power forward must be able to bump and grind, come up with loose pucks, play the boards in his own zone, create room for other players," Pleau says. "But he's also able to create offense, finish off the play. He can cause commotion, draws traffic to himself."

It is possible to draw a composite profile of a power forward. A power forward should be able to meet the following criteria:

Size Does Matter

At a minimum, a power forward should weigh 215 pounds, though it's more desirable to be 220. That's not to say that a 210-pound player couldn't be a power forward, as long as he had other qualities of a power forward. The point is that it would be impossible for Theo Fleury to be considered a power forward at his size, even though he's a tenacious and rough package. A power forward must be able to mete out punishment and be capable of physical intimidation, which is far easier for a man with size to accomplish.

Philadelphia Flyers captain Eric Lindros, airborne in this picture, might be the prototype of the twenty-first century National Hockey League player. He's a 240-pound center with a monstrous style along the boards and a high-tempo finesse in the open ice.

Eating Their Spinach

Power forwards have Popeye builds with bulging biceps and anvil-sized forearms. Gordie Howe was probably the last man who could be a legitimate power forward without considering the weight room his second home. A power forward has to be strong enough to avoid being moved out of the front of the net, and big enough to make defensemen think twice about going into the corner with him.

Angel Wings Disallowed

It's impossible to put a penalty minute minimum on a power forward, because it's necessary to keep him on the ice. But no Lady Byng candidates qualify for the power forward status. Part of being a power forward "is never having to say you're sorry." A power forward must play on the outside edges of the game's rules. A power forward must have a pinch of hatred in his soul, especially when it comes to losing. A power forward must have a large supply of sticks because he will break them over his knee, the boards, or a large defenseman when things aren't going his team's way.

Tough Guy at Heart

Coaches don't want their power forward to do much fighting, but they want him to be proficient when he does. A power forward should at least give the impression that he can whip all comers even if he only drops his gloves twice a season. The aura of intimidation is a key component of a power forward's package. He may need to snap once or twice a season just to plant a constant seed of doubt in a defenseman's mind that this might be the night he is going to go postal.

As the NHL prepares for hockey in the twenty-first century, greater pressure is being placed on scouts to find potential power forwards. Bigger players, particularly bigger players with speed or skill, get more second chances from coaches than their average-sized counterparts. When a big guy makes a mistake, he will get hockey's version of a mulligan from his coach. He will get chance after chance to make the big hit, while the smaller player needs to be perfect from the beginning.

"One of our goals is for all tough guys to become power forwards," says Nashville general manager David Poile. "That's why we take chances on the big guys. Darren McCarty is probably the ultimate example of what can happen." McCarty began as one of the league's top fighters, and has now evolved into one of the league's power forwards.

Coaches are far more patient with bigger players, knowing that the day when an average player is 6-foot-2, 215 pounds, is not that far away. "When I played I weighed two hundred pounds, and I was considered a pretty big player," says agent Tom Laidlaw, a former player who retired in 1989-90. "If I was still playing I think I would have trouble handling some of the bigger players."

Right wing Cam Neely's maturation into a 225-pound, 55-goal scorer in 1989-90 seemed to trigger an even keener NHL interest in players with size. The NHL had long been interested in bigger players, but they began to look under more rocks for big players after Neely began dominating. The left wings who had to defend against Neely couldn't handle him. The left defensemen felt like they were wrestling with a grizzly bear. Goaltenders couldn't believe that a player Neely's size was so nimble around the net.

"He never had two hands on his stick. He could grab a defenseman with his free hand and throw him down," says former NHL goaltender Darren Pang. "Then he would maneuver around in front of the net and go up over your glove hand. That was an impossible combination to deal with."

Phoenix Coyotes winger Rick Tocchet also holds the reputation as a player who is valuable as both a physical intimidator and an offensive threat. "He's the kind who can be playing with a broken jaw and still throw an elbow in the face of a defenseman, knock down the goalie, and then score in the empty net at a clutch time of the game," Pang says.

Phoenix Coyotes captain Keith Tkachuk is a throwback to the 1950s, when the leading scorer was usually the roughest player. Gordie Howe, Maurice "Rocket" Richard, and Milt Schmidt were captains who could score, hit, fight, and control the game in any number of ways. Tkachuk is the 1990s version, right down to his willingness to do whatever it takes to be successful. "His intensity and focus are contagious,'" says Ron Wilson, who coached Tkachuk at the World Cup.

Tkachuk plays the game with the same level of fire as guys like Howe, Richard, and even Mark Messier. NHL goalkeepers needed a

Phoenix Coyotes right wing Rick Tocchet, right, is checked by Philadelphia defenseman Chris Therien. Tocchet has been among the league's most respected power forwards for many years.

flame-retardant psyche to face Richard—"The Rocket"—when the game was on the line. His fiery eyes scorched an opponent's confidence even before he unleashed his wickedly accurate shot. Many succumbed quickly to his reputation as a respected leader and multiple championship winner with a résumé full of game-winning goals. Richard had elbows as sharp as a Bowie knife, and fists that could crush like a jackhammer. He had the lion's heart, the shark's soul, and the eagle's ability to soar higher and more magnificently than most.

Curiously, this description fits Messier as well. Although Messier and Richard didn't play the same position, they are soul mates in their ability to humble opponents. Messier is a center and Richard was a right wing, but Messier has played wing in the past with the same level of viciousness as the Rocket. They will be linked through the ages by their competitiveness and the forceful way they dominated the game. It wasn't their success that intimidated foes; it was how they achieved that success. They were like fighter pilots, always pushing the envelope. If they were distance runners, they would have been the kind of athletes who ran the final mile faster than any previous mile. If they were Indy car drivers, they would have driven within millimeters of the wall to mount a final passing charge to win a race. If they were boxers, they would have been knockout artists.

"The Rocket was a finisher," says St. Louis Blues vice president Ron Caron, who started his career as a Canadiens scout in the 1950s. "He was like the boxer who faced a ten-round fight with the idea: 'Don't waste my time with the first nine rounds. I'm going to win it now.'"

Messier is faster and more skillful with the puck, but Richard was still a strong skater for his era. Messier owns six championship rings, five earned with the Edmonton Oilers and one with the New York Rangers. Richard won seven with the Montreal Canadiens. Messier ranks second all-time with 295 playoff points, and Richard's name is constantly in the NHL playoff record book. Coming into the 1998-99 season, Messier had more than 600 goals in 18 seasons and Richard had 544 in 18 seasons. Messier guaranteed, and then delivered, an important victory with a brilliant performance against the New Jersey Devils in the 1994 playoffs. Richard shares the league record of five goals in a playoff game, set in a 5-1 win against Toronto in 1943-44, and holds the NHL record of six overtime playoff goals. "When they would ask (general manager Frank) Selke who was going to score in overtime, he would always say Richard. Most of the time he was right," Caron remembers.

Richard was a left-handed shot who played right wing, and Messier is a left-handed shot who likes to cruise in on the right side and unleash his drive. They differ there because Richard liked to use a backhander, perhaps because maskless goaltenders had a difficult time judging the height of a backhander, which instilled another element of fear in them. "Messier and Richard could both play a little mean," says former New Jersey and Washington general manager Max McNab, who played against Richard in the late 1940s and early 1950s.

Like Messier, the Rocket never set his phasers on stun. He dialed up for big games, and opponents got hurt if they were in his path. He was a tough, powerful man who intimidated opponents physically as well as psychologically. He strived to be victorious by any means necessary, even if it meant charging around some of the rules. Richard had 1,285 penalty minutes, compared to Messier's 1,596.

"Most great players are tremendously smart players, and Richard was a smart player," says Hall of Fame goaltender Glenn Hall. "He was a great educator of goaltenders. I didn't like the fact that he educated me as much as he did."

Like Richard, Howe's style relied as much on his brain as his brawn. He knew how to effectively use his strength as a weapon.

Howe recognized the importance of intimidation. We dare not compare Gordie Howe's accomplishments with those of any other mortal, current, past, or future. He should forever be called the "Incomparable Gordie Howe" in terms of his hockey accomplishments. His name was synonymous with hockey long before Wayne Gretzky was even born.

Eric Lindros isn't in Howe's league in terms of accomplishment, but he is the player today who comes closest to matching Howe in terms of size, physical dominance, and playing style. The Philadelphia Flyers gave up Peter Forsberg, Steve Duchesne, Kerry Huffman, Mike Ricci, Ron Hextall, Chris Simon, and two first-round draft picks, plus $15 million, to acquire Lindros from Quebec in 1992. The Flyers believed Lindros was the second coming of Howe, a player capable of taking charge all over the ice. Lindros won a Hart Trophy in 1995, but hasn't been able to match Howe's durability yet.

The unifying element of Lindros and Howe is that they are big, powerful, offensive players who control the puck like small, crafty centermen. Both players' skating processes caught defensemen by surprise. They never seemed to be going as fast as they were. To defensemen, trying to wrap their arms around a Howe or a Lindros is like trying to put a saddle on a charging elephant. It's a task not easily accomplished without bruising and swelling.

"What's funny now is that I remember when Howe played he looked 6-foot-8, and we thought he should be playing basketball," Glenn Hall says. "Now when I look at him, he seems like he's as small as (5-foot-7) Theo Fleury. That's how much bigger the players are now."

It will be difficult for any modern NHL player to come close to matching the impact Howe had as a power forward in the 1950s, 1960s, and 1970s. As an offensive performer, he controlled the tempo of almost all of his games, particularly in the pre-Orr days when

Underrated New York Islanders hitter Rich Pilon topples Philadelphia's Eric Lindros in a game in 1994-95. Islanders goaltender Jamie McLennan also paid a price for this hit when Lindros fell on top of him. Offensive players don't try too hard to avoid goaltenders when they are knocked down in the crease area.

defensemen weren't wandering up the ice to make plays. Howe would use his strength, size, skill, and nastiness to take charge of the offensive zone. He netted twenty-five or more goals for twenty-two consecutive seasons in an era when twenty goals defined stardom. He won six scoring championships and led the league in goals five times. He won the Hart Trophy as MVP six times. Gordie Howe was to hockey what Babe Ruth was to baseball.

Howe had puck skills that others did not, such as the ability to shoot with either hand. Although he was a right-handed shot, Howe could quickly turn a misguided centering feed into a goal by simply shooting the puck left-handed.

"He probably got fifty or sixty goals in his career like that," says former NHL goaltender Eddie Johnston. "A puck would be in his skates and he would kick it to the wrong side. Then he would shoot it left-handed and it would catch you by surprise. Nobody else could do that."

Possessing the league's hardest wrist shot, Howe could launch a rising shot from the high slot that would simply terrorize a maskless goaltender. With Howe's powerful stride, he was frequently able to roar past a defenseman. Goaltenders in that era remember getting torched often from twenty feet. But Howe would also drive the net, an effective strategy to use against undersized blueliners who weren't physically accessorized to handle a player of his size and skill level. "He was a bull," Johnston remembered. "If there was no room, he would try to jam on you and drive you and the puck into the net."

Howe's intimidation quotient was stratospheric, raised to that elevation by a series of physical confrontations capped by a memorable fight against New York Rangers' Lou Fontinato, at New York's Madison Square Garden on February 1, 1959. Many heavyweight boxing

Players encircle Gordie Howe and Lou Fontinato as they battle in one of the greatest fights in NHL history. Howe's reputation as a rough competitor was bolstered by his overwhelming victory in this scrap.

matches hosted by the Garden over the years haven't matched the ferocity of the Fontinato-Howe tussle.

According to newspaper reports at the time, the scrap started over the Red Wings' rough treatment of young Rangers winger Eddie Shack. Early in the game, Detroit's Pete Goegan smacked Shack so hard against the boards that he broke the Plexiglas. Later, as the Rangers were building a 4-1 lead, Howe cut Shack with his stick. Shack needed three stitches to repair the wound.

Fontinato and Howe had fought before. In fact, Fontinato still had a scar from the twelve stitches he earned by fighting Howe in a previous brawl. But as one of the league's toughest fighters and the Rangers' "policeman," Fontinato made it a point to tell Howe that if he touched Shack again, he would have an appointment with

Fontinato, a burly twenty-seven-year-old 195-pounder with a jackhammer punch.

Moments later, Howe and Shack collided behind the net. Fontinato took his cue. He confronted Howe and the gloves were dropped. Punches started flying and about a minute later Howe, then thirty-one, emerged with a reputation that would serve him well for the next two decades.

GORDIE HOWE

Gordie Howe could forever hold the title of the most incredible physical specimen to play in the National Hockey League.

When Howe started with the Detroit Red Wings in 1946, the league had never before seen a 205-pound player who could play the game with such amazing skill. The Floral, Saskatchewan, native never lifted a weight in his life, and yet he was as strong as anyone who had ever played the game. His wrist shot was like an artillery discharge. Before the days of radar guns and electronic timing, someone used physics to calculate his wrist shot to be at least one hundred miles per hour.

Whether you believe that or not, it's impossible to argue with the fact that the strength of his wrists was far above the norm. He was a right-handed shot who thought nothing of shifting his straight stick in his hands and firing a shot left-handed. "He was nature's biggest mistake," says his one-time linemate Max McNab.

"Players like him come along once in a lifetime."

Howe's package also included a leathery toughness that allowed him to play through pain and injury. What separates Howe from other impressive physical specimens is his durability and longevity. His NHL and World Hockey Association career lasted from 1946-47 to 1979-80. The only concession Howe ever made to his age was his decision to play lighter in his final years. His former coach Harry Neale remembers that Howe played exactly four pounds lighter in his thirty-second NHL season than he did in his first NHL campaign. At fifty, he was among the WHA's top scorers with ninety-six points. He turned fifty-two in his final NHL season and managed a respectable total of fifteen goals. He also had forty-two penalty minutes, a clear indication that he never changed his approach to the game. Howe only reached one hundred penalty minutes four times in his career, mostly

According to the news reports, Howe grabbed Fontinato's sweater and tagged him multiple times with savage uppercuts to the face. Estimates of the length of the fight differed wildly even among those who had witnessed it, ranging from thirty seconds to four minutes. But the best guess is that the scrap lasted less than sixty seconds. Fontinato's face, particularly around his nose, was a bloody mess. In a salute to the machismo of the time, Fontinato

because opponents were fearful of riling him up. He had only fifty-seven minutes in 1952-53 when he won his third consecutive scoring title, and yet most of his opponents probably felt like Howe had accumulated more than one hundred minutes. As one of the league's top stars, he couldn't afford to be off the ice too often. He picked his spots to throw an elbow or a punch. His penalty minutes didn't always reflect how rough he played or how intimidating he really was.

By today's standards, Howe would be just an average-sized player. But one should remember that if Howe were playing today, he would have undoubtedly been in the weight room. With the improved training methods, Howe might have played at 220 pounds, and probably would have been able to bench press a refrigerator.

Neale says he has never encountered an athlete with Howe's natural level of conditioning, strength, and desire. Howe did have some limita-

tions: he wasn't able to run at age fifty, although he made an attempt. Neale insisted that his players be able to run two miles before they came to the New England Whalers training camp in 1977-78. In acknowledgement of Howe's age and stature, Neale told him he didn't have to run the race. But Howe was concerned about how it would look to the others players on the team. He ran for the first couple of days, and his ankles and shins were becoming quite sore. Neale decided that it wasn't a good idea for Howe to run, but Howe was still concerned about how it would look to his teammates if he didn't do everything they did.

Neale told him not to worry. He called all of the players together for a "special announcement."

"Gordie Howe no longer has to run," Neale said. "And I'm making a deal with all of you. If you play with me in the season you turn fifty, you won't have to run either."

finished the game, even though his nose formed an unnatural forty-five-degree angle with his face. According to newspaper reports, his snout was so badly mashed that surgery was required to make it functional. Howe dislocated a finger in the fight and suffered a gash over his eye.

Inspired by the Howe triumph, the Red Wings came back to win the game. But more importantly, Howe established himself as the league's toughest player. Before, everyone had been leery of Howe. After the fight, the word around the league was: avoid Howe at all costs.

"Defensemen never liked playing against him because he always had his elbows in their kisser," Johnston remembers. "And the messages he sent out early in his career with that fight against Fontinato had an effect. Everyone said: 'Let's not wake him up.'"

Hall of Fame coach Scotty Bowman remembers Howe didn't fight much later in his career, mostly because no one wanted to challenge him. Smart men presumably believe it isn't worth the risk to challenge the league's top gunslinger.

"But every once in a while he would do something just to remind you," Bowman says. "He was feared."

The amazing aspect of Howe's "bad hombre" reputation is that most teammates and opponents who got to know him later in life found him to be a gentle-souled person. "He is one of the classiest men I've ever met," says Johnston. "And what an ambassador he's been for the game."

Howe certainly didn't have a reputation for being gentle in the Original Six days. Teams played each other quite regularly and players knew the tendencies of every player in the league. Stan Mikita, who was a small, prickly player when he came into the NHL, has told the story many times of how, as a young player, he high-sticked

Howe. Guys on the bench immediately told him to keep his head up, and to make sure he knew where Howe was at all times when he was on the ice.

Nothing happened in that game, and afterward a cocky Mikita told teammates that perhaps they had overstated Howe's reputation. As far as Mikita was concerned, Howe seemed more like a pussy-cat in that game, and not the tiger that he was reputed to be.

A few games later, when Mikita had forgotten about Howe, Howe skated by, cut Mikita with his stick, and finished him off with an elbow. "That was for what happened three games ago," Howe reportedly said.

As Howe grew older, he didn't need to tangle very often with established players, having earned his right-of-way in the preceding seasons. But he made a special point of providing rookies with a greeting that spelled out precisely what was expected of them in terms of his right to skate up and down his wing unimpeded.

"I remember Tim Ecclestone (1967-68 to 1977-78) was twenty years old and playing his first NHL game and Gordie gives him three elbows," says former St. Louis player Bob Plager. "'Welcome to the NHL, kid.' He tested every rookie. He straightened them out and he got plenty of room."

Howe told more than one teammate that he considered his stick "the great equalizer." When he got a chance to play with his sons in the WHA, he was like an old lion protecting his cubs. "When they attacked his sons, he went after them," Plager says. "People feared Gordie."

Howe's son Marty, who played on the same team with his father in the WHA days, says that one of the keys to Howe's longevity was the fact that he "never lost his edge."

"It didn't matter whether he knew you or not," Marty says. "He would still cut you."

Marty says his father based his personal justice system on what was being done to him at the time. He would leave an opponent alone as long as the opponent didn't violate one of his rules.

"You didn't make him look stupid," Marty recalls. "If you tried to make him look stupid, you would get hit with a stick real quick. He didn't like getting hooked from behind in the ribs. He had busted his ribs so many times that that used to aggravate him. If you did that, you got the stick or the elbow, depending upon how close you were. In front of the net, defensemen like to hold (a forward's) stick because then you know where they are without looking. If you did that, he would start to skate away like most people do, but then the stick would come back and he would try to take your chin off."

Howe never forgot about settling the score, but always mixed a bit of graciousness with his viciousness. "I think he learned that from all of these people who ran at him over the years," Harry Neale says. "When you played against him, you would say, 'Look at that dirty bastard.' But when he was on your team, you would laugh at how he would deal with people."

Neale remembers his team playing against Howe in a playoff series. It was a rough series and Howe's stick and elbows were up as high as anyone else's. Even as pro hockey's all-time leading scorer at the time, he wouldn't put himself above doing the dirty work. That's what makes a great power forward.

"Through that series he kept cutting guys and skating to the bench yelling that he was sorry," Neale says. "Right, I'm sorry this is the 900th guy I cut in my career."

Even though today's NHL boasts more power forwards roaming the ice than there were in Howe's era, the enlarged field hasn't produced one as menacing as he was.

CHAPTER FIVE

Disturbers of the Peace

AGITATORS

The players with the dirtiest jobs in the NHL are also those who can claim the most vulgar job descriptions in pro sports history. They are called "shit disturbers." And that's actually an apt portrayal of the work they do for successful teams.

They are called "agitators" in more polite conversation, though the name really doesn't do justice to their role. These guys are the trolls of hockey—players willing to play ugly, to get down in the slime, if necessary, to help their teams win. They can be trash talkers, wrist slashers, or star abusers. They'll talk raunchily about your mother, demean your sister, or slice open your favorite teammate if that is what gets you off your game. At best, they are annoying. At worst, they are like killer bees, forever anxious to deliver their stingers.

These guys have been around forever, and like cockroaches, they aren't likely to ever go away. They are too valuable. Today's agitators, such as New York's Theo Fleury and former Ranger Esa Tikkanen, Colorado's Claude Lemieux, Detroit's Kirk Maltby and Kris Draper, Buffalo's Mike Peca, and St. Louis' Geoff Courtnall, among others, are as valuable as big hitters or goal scorers. Opponents are so busy being annoyed by these guys that they lose their concentration.

The patron saint of all agitators may be Bryan Watson, a pesky player who infuriated star offensive players—in particular, Chicago's Bobby Hull—with his antics in the 1960s. Watson was assigned to follow Hull all over the ice, and do absolutely everything he could think of to harass him.

In those days, Hull refused to even talk about Watson because he said Watson "had gained too much publicity" at Hull's expense.

"When Watson and Glen Sather were playing in Pittsburgh they drove us all nuts," says former St. Louis player Bob Plager. "You could not skate by the Pittsburgh bench without those two having something to say."

Plager would yell at them: "When you are on the ice, we'll go."

"Oh, we will be on next shift," Watson would reply.

But the agitator usually doesn't intend to fight because it's only his job to rile up the opposition, "to stir up some shit," as players would say. The best at their trade are those who can stir up trouble and not get caught up in it when it boils over.

"Those kinds of players are usually good players and you don't want them off the ice," says former NHL player Tom Laidlaw. "He has to be a good athlete to be a real disturber because if you can catch one and beat the hell out of him it defeats their purpose."

Needless to say, agitators aren't the most well-liked players in the league, although they are usually popular with teammates. Lemieux in particular seems to have a large number of acquaintances who would like to pop him. Yet Lemieux is considered one of the league's most coveted playoff performers.

Laidlaw remembers that even as a rookie, Lemieux's mouth was always going. In the 1986 Stanley Cup semifinals, Laidlaw attempted to hit Lemieux, who saw him coming and lowered his shoulder to deaden Laidlaw's charge. Laidlaw went down in a heap.

"What's the matter?" rookie Lemieux asked Laidlaw. "Did you run into a wall?"

The next time he was down the ice, Laidlaw raised his stick to

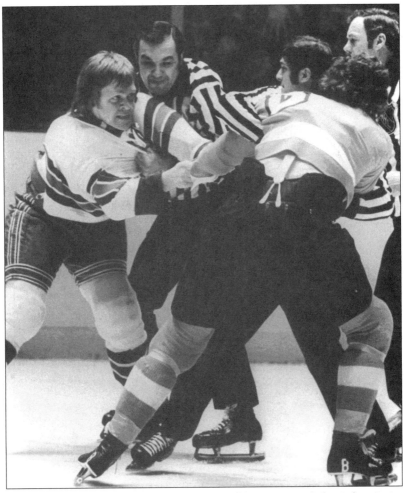

Glen Sather (left), shown here battling Philadelphia's Dave Schultz in the 1970s, was regarded as one of the league's top agitators. Today, he's remembered as the architect of the Edmonton Oilers' five Stanley Cup championships in the 1980s. He's currently the Oilers' president and general manager.

catch Lemieux across the face. "What's the matter? Did you run into a fence?" Laidlaw asked in his best imitation of Lemieux's French accent.

Lemieux has had dozens upon dozens of similar run-ins with players around the league, but even he may not be able to match the level of trouble Esa Tikkanen has stirred up in his career. Tikkanen has gained much of his notoriety by being one of the league's best shadows. In one game against Pittsburgh, he did something to get Mario Lemieux to take a swing at him.

"I just asked how his Mum was doing," Tikkanen said after the game, with a grin on his face.

Esa Tikkanen drives opponents crazy in the playoffs in multiple languages. He can talk trash in English, Finnish, and what former Edmonton teammates used to call "Tikkish." That's a combination of Finnish and English uttered so fast that it is almost unintelligible, although opponents can tell from Tikkanen's grin and expression that they probably wouldn't like the words even if they understood them. He's a scrappy, defensive-minded forward who can shut down the opponent's top scorer and still score a big goal. He has seventy-two playoff goals, including nine for the Rangers in the 1997 playoffs.

"If you are talking about a dirty dozen, Esa has to be captain," says ESPN analyst Bill Clement.

The most unlikely agitator in the league is Mike Peca, who looks much more like Clark Kent than an NHL playoff Superman. Wearing a suit and horn-rim glasses, Peca looks like he would prefer to be trading stocks in a bull market rather than trading jabs with a bullish defenseman. "But underneath that Wall Street exterior is the Tasmanian devil who can't wait to get on the ice," says Bill Clement.

He's always on the ice against the league's top offensive stars, and he's not shy about punishing his opponents. When he was playing for Vancouver, he crushed Teemu Selanne with a hit that let everyone in the league know he plays hockey like it's a declared war. Peca is a clean-cut man with a spicy playing style. He's a thorn in the side of most of the top skilled players. Dominik Hasek is undeniably the Sabres' most important player, but Peca's performance will

Colorado's Claude Lemieux (No. 22) exchanges words with New Jersey Devils captain Scott Stevens during a regular-season clash. The fact that Stevens is a former teammate makes no difference to Lemieux, who has earned a reputation as one of the league's most disliked irritants. If he annoys an opponent to the point of taking a penalty, Lemieux feels he has done his job.

always be a determining factor in how far Buffalo advances in the playoffs.

"I don't think you can measure how valuable a guy like Peca is. Obviously, the idea is to make sure you neutralize the other team's top weapon, and he does it as well as anybody."

Peca, twenty-four, has been using this style since he realized as a rookie that grittiness is next to godliness in NHL circles. As a rookie with the Vancouver Canucks in 1994-95, he remembers doing a good checking job against Jeremy Roenick's line in Chicago.

"I still think to this day that it was some of the best hockey I've ever played," Peca says. "I think at that moment I realized how effective that style can be."

He has a mental notebook on how players react to his style of play. "It bothers some more than others," Peca says. "There are always certain levels of frustration. Some want to get back physically and others try to elevate their game to get a goal."

It's not surprising that Peca seems more effective in the play-offs, when the pressure is so intense it drips off players.

"The stock of prickly players rises in the playoffs because refs respect the jobs they have to do, so they let them play a little more prickly," Clement says. "I'm not talking about obstruction. I'm talking the in-your-face stuff. That's why a guy like Mike Peca can do even better work in the playoffs."

In close games, Peca's style grates even more on players. While they are fretting about him, he's thinking about scoring. Clement says Peca is one of the league's most competitive players: "It's not like he has to wind himself up."

Some of the best agitators are a cross between a pit bull and a greyhound. It's difficult to be an agitator unless you skate well enough to stay up with the top players. You have to get close enough to whisper in their ear, or to give them some love taps with your stick. That's why speedy Kirk Maltby is gaining notoriety for his ability to drive opponents bonkers.

Whenever there's a scrum of players pushing along the boards, Maltby is in the middle, pushing and making a general nuisance of himself. One of his goals is to make the opponent worry about him more than about what's happening in the game. "He's an aggravating player to play against because he's in there hacking and whacking," says Detroit general manager Ken Holland. "He finishes his checks. He's always right on top of you."

Another agitator who drives players to distraction is Geoff Courtnall, although he's also known as a goal scorer. But calling Courtnall a goal scorer is selling him many stitches short. Come play-off time, he uses his mouth and irritating presence as much as his goal-scoring knack.

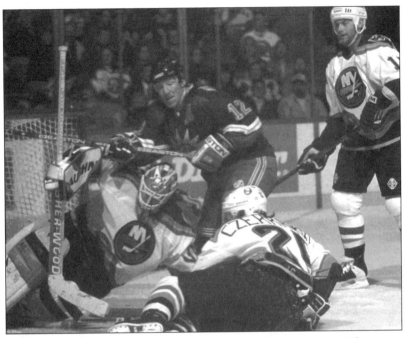

The area in front of the net is a major battleground in every game. Mike Keane is man who can survive the hand-to-hand encounters that occur in what could be called hockey's version of "no-man's land." Keane is among the league's most grating agitators.

Overlooked in his recent thirty-goal season is the fact that he's a very unpleasant opponent. As noteworthy as 109 career playoff points in 156 games is the fact that he has 262 career playoff penalty minutes. He earned a total of fifty-one minutes when he helped Vancouver make the Stanley Cup final in 1994.

"Al MacInnis told me that when he played in Calgary, Courtnall was always bugging him, always getting in his face," Blues general manager Larry Pleau says, laughing.

Courtnall is fast enough to track down anyone on the ice, and he likes to violate a player's personal space. He's not really a fighter as much as an instigator. Think of Courtnall as the kid who used to

The St. Louis Blues' Geoff Courtnall gives a face wash to an opposing Dallas Stars player. Courtnall's importance to his team is really threefold: he has speed, he can score goals, and he can distract opponents with his irritating presence.

knock down the wasp nest in the schoolyard just to see what would happen. "He's always charging the net," Pleau says. "He's always drawing penalties. He's always putting himself in a position that someone has to get a piece of him. He either gets through them, or he aggravates them, or he gets that penalty."

There are other players in the league who are borderline disturbers, but don't earn the title for one reason or another. Dallas Stars winger Mike Keane probably would be considered an agitator, if not for the fact that he sticks around to fight too often. But he might be as irritating to play against as any player in the league. In the 1998 playoffs, he laid out Detroit tough guy Darren McCarty with a check that was as hard as any hit recorded that season. "Mike believes that no matter how big the obstacle is, it's capable of being defeated," says teammate Brian Skrudland, who also played in Montreal with Keane.

Dallas Stars coach Ken Hitchcock remembers coaching against him in junior hockey in the mid-1980s. "He really liked the game when it heated up," Hitchcock says. "The harder it got, the better he got."

Keane, who is about 5-foot-11, 185 pounds, contends that he's not the same player he was in junior hockey. "Believe it or not, I was a fighter back then," he says. "I don't fight much any more."

But he still irritates opponents like fingernails down a chalkboard. "He's not in the same mold as Claude Lemieux, but he's right around there," Craig Ludwig says.

Theo Fleury is a better example of the disturber because at 5-foot-7, 160 pounds, he's not a candidate to be trading punches with the heavyweights. But he has probably triggered as many melees as his teammates have. He's always sticking his nose into what's happening on the ice. He's always got something to say, much of it not printable in the newspaper, and he's very aggravating. Tom Laidlaw remembers wanting to lay out Theo Fleury. "But I could never catch him," Laidlaw says.

WAYNE GRETZKY

Wayne Gretzky's status as the NHL's all-time leading scorer hasn't given him immunity from persecution on the NHL ice rinks.

Even though Gretzky has won the Lady Byng Trophy as the league's most gentlemanly player five times, he's actually been assessed three fighting majors during an NHL career that spans almost two full decades. He's also endured his fair share of big hits.

Former NHL coach Harry Neale says one of the hardest hits he's ever seen was delivered to a young Gretzky by a player named Bill McCreary, who played only twelve NHL games for the Toronto Maple Leafs in 1980-81.

"I'm sure no one has hit Gretzky any harder," Neale says. "It was a thundering bodycheck. It might have been an accidental collision that turned into a hit at the last second."

As a fighter, Gretzky didn't stray from his weight class. When he was a rookie in 1979-80, the 175-pound Gretzky had a bout with 179-pound Doug Lecuyer. In 1982-83, he dropped his gloves to spar with 165-pound Neal Broten, and in 1983-84, he scrapped with Chicago's 180-pound Bob Murray.

The scrap with Murray was his most memorable bout. "I swung at him and he blocked it and knocked me down," Gretzky recalls. "He said: 'Had enough?' I said, 'Yes,' and that was the fight."

What does Gretzky think about when he's watching others fight? "I think I'm glad it's not me," he says.

(Above) New Jersey Devils player Kevin Dean (No. 28) obviously isn't buying into the myth that Wayne Gretzky wasn't touched in his NHL career.

(Opposite) Wayne Gretzky (No. 99) was elusive enough to avoid many checks in his career, yet he endured his fair share of rough treatment.

CHAPTER SIX

Take Me Out to the Brawl Game

FIGHTING

Long-time fans would swear that in the 1970s the National Hockey League was sometimes like the old Wild West, where lawlessness was rampant and top gunslingers carried the day.

NHL officials won't argue. Former referee Bryan Lewis remembers the night in Oakland in 1975-76 when California defenseman Mike Christie made the mistake of doing something the Philadelphia Flyers didn't like. (The Oakland/California Seals lasted from 1967-68 until 1975-76 before moving to Cleveland.) Lewis thought Christie's debt to the Flyers was paid after winger Don Saleski pounded him in a fight. But Christie's nightmare had only just begun. Even after Christie was escorted to the penalty box, he had no relief from the Flyers' assault. A gang of Flyers jumped him in the box, and a bewildered Christie was forced to fight them off like a U.S. Marine defending a foxhole. Lewis recalled that Jim Neilson was the only California player to come directly to Christie's aid. Lewis has a photograph of himself sitting on the boards writing down the numbers of the offending Flyers for the purpose of awarding penalties.

"I hate to compare the Flyers to a pack of wolves, but they certainly took care of each other," Lewis remembers. "To (Philadelphia captain) Bobby Clarke's credit, he's the one who said that's it. He said, 'Let him get off the ice.' The seas parted and Christie was able to get off the ice."

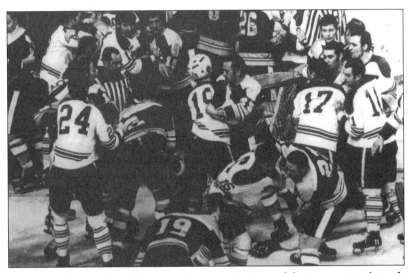

This bench-clearing brawl between the Boston Bruins and the Toronto Maple Leafs on February 1, 1970, wasn't uncommon in that era. The NHL discouraged bench-clearing brawls in 1977-78 when it instituted a rule making it an automatic ejection for the third man in a fight. The bench-clearing brawl was eliminated for good in 1987-88 when the league imposed a ten-game suspension for the first player off the bench to join a brawl, and a possible suspension for his coach.

The next night Lewis had the misfortune of being assigned to the Philadelphia-Vancouver game. Prepared for another war, Lewis was rather surprised when back-up goaltender Bobby Taylor skated by him during the pregame warm-up. "Don't worry," Taylor said, laughing. "They've put seat belts on the benches so we can't get off."

Philadelphia's Broad Street Bullies' team set a vicious cadence in the early to mid-1970s, and the rest of the league followed suit. "The league let them play that way," says former NHL goaltender John Davidson. "You could have given them their first penalty six seconds into the game and kept the penalty box filled the whole game."

The tragedy of that style of play is that it created a reputation that the league has never been able to erase, even though there haven't been many nights of mayhem in recent years. The last bench-clearing brawl took place in the 1986-87 playoffs, when the Montreal Canadiens and the Philadelphia Flyers squared off in a pregame all-hands-on-deck scrap.

Some still argue that the league's national growth has been stunted by its unwillingness to legislate fighting completely out of the game, but even they admit that fighting is far more controlled than it was a couple of decades ago. The power of fighters was weakened by several pieces of owners' legislation, including the two-minute instigator penalty for the player who initiates the fight. Other important rule changes include the expulsion of the third man to join a fight and the mandatory ten-game suspension for the first player who leaves the bench to join a fight, plus a possible suspension (at the discretion of the commissioner) for the offending player's coach.

Players probably think more today about starting a fight than they did in the 1970s or before. Because the stakes are higher now that the television contracts are larger, corporate sponsorship is richer, and player salaries have increased, coaches are less forgiving of tough guys who don't think through the time and place of each bout. "Players in my role have to be a lot more disciplined and a lot less reckless than they were in the past because there is great parity in the league," says Mighty Ducks of Anaheim tough guy Stu Grimson. "When you put your team in a vulnerable position (by giving up power play opportunities) you run the risk of losing a game. When you put yourself in that kind of position on a regular basis, it makes a dramatic difference in the standings."

As a result, the heavyweight has become primarily a defensive, rather than an offensive, weapon. "We are almost a police presence, more than anything," Grimson says.

In the days of the Original Six teams, the top fighter from every team was referred to as the team's "policeman," because his primary

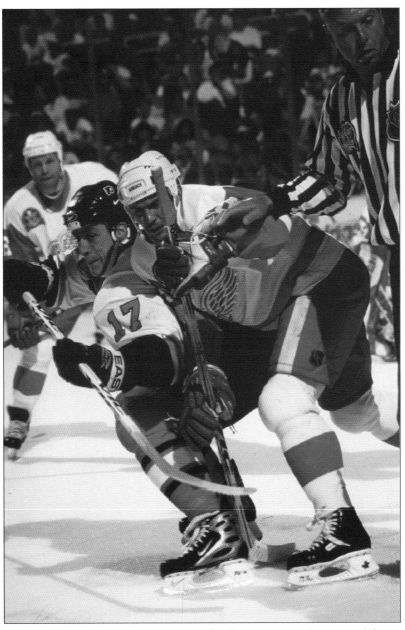

Philadelphia's Rod Brind'Amour is shoved hard into the corner by Detroit defense-man Jamie Pushor.

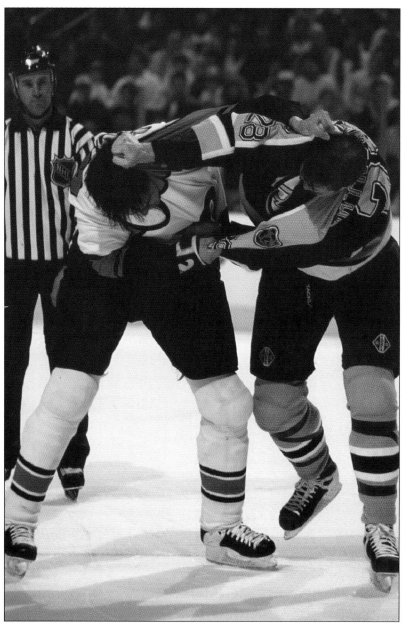

Hair pulling will earn a player a gross misconduct penalty, and these two combatants look as if they could be in danger of getting that call.

With three 300+ penalty-minute seasons to his credit, Gino Odjick has earned his place among the league's top heavyweights. Odjick is an Algonquin Indian who began his career on outdoor rinks on the Maniwaki Indian Reserve. He grew up admiring the playing style of feisty Boston player Stan Jonathan. He's never listed among the best punchers, although he's held his own against the league's best scrappers. He set the Vancouver Canucks' record of 370 penalty minutes for a season in 1991-92 when he was among the league leaders with 31 fights. Most top heavyweights today average about twenty to twenty-four bouts per season.

One hockey myth is that no one ever gets hurt in a fight. Toronto's Nick Kypreos, shown here lying on the ice, had to retire after getting knocked out during a fight with New York Rangers' Ryan VandenBussch (shown here being led away by officials). Kypreos hit his head on the ice when he went down.

Fighting still plays a role in the NHL, but it has become relatively insignificant in the postseason. In the 1999 playoffs, there were only eight fights in eighty-six games.

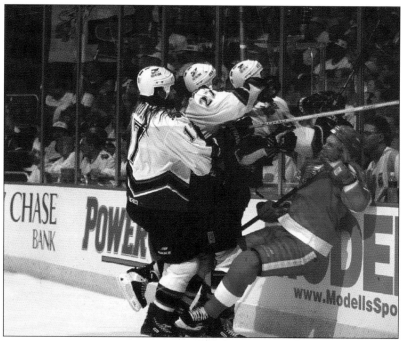

Chris Simon seems to have a cult following somewhat like what Dennis Rodman has in the NBA. Simon isn't as exotic as Rodman, but Simon's Native American heritage and long black hair have given him a popular signature. Although most in the hockey world view Tony Twist as the heavyweight champion, Simon usually wins many fan polls as the toughest player in hockey. He's popular with his home fans, and many in Colorado say Simon's trade to Washington has hurt the Avalanche more than they will admit. Simon has a rebellious streak in him—proven by his confrontations with coach Marc Crawford in Colorado and now Ron Wilson in Washington. These confrontations may stem from the fact that coaches usually want more out of Simon—a player who has the potential to be a scorer as well as a fighter.

Battles in front of the net earn power forwards their reputations as warriors. Here, New Jersey's Bobby Holik, right, fights back against New York Rangers defenseman Ulf Samuelsson, who is attempting to clear him out of the crease area.

Former Detroit Red Wings center Keith Primeau, now with Carolina, is sandwiched by a pair of New York Islanders.

purpose was to protect teammates and give some law and order to rough-and-tumble games. In the 1970s, fighters were called "goons." Now, fighters are referred to as simply "tough guys" or "enforcers." They live in a world where the decision to fight can be more complicated than the fight itself. Here are some reasons why a heavyweight will fight:

White Knight

When a team's top offensive player gets rammed hard into the boards, the heavyweight will mete out punishment to the opposing team or player. The message is clear: you can't play rough with my skilled players.

How the punishment is exacted doesn't always follow the same script. If the Washington Capitals target St. Louis center Pierre Turgeon for extra physical attention, the St. Louis Blues tough guys probably won't call out Craig Berube to teach the Capitals a lesson. Instead, Blues tough guy Kelly Chase might smack Peter Bondra hard along the boards. "You will still probably have the confrontation with Craig Berube anyway, but you've let them know not to take liberties on our offensive players," Chase says. The Berube-Chase battle would simply tie up loose ends.

Black Knight

Even under the tighter rules, some players occasionally use their toughness in an attempt to intimidate or goad the other team's player into reaction penalties. Although intimidation doesn't play the role it once did, it is clearly still part of the game.

When Anaheim superstar Paul Kariya suffered a season-ending concussion after being cross-checked by Gary Suter during the 1997-98 season, the Mighty Ducks responded by acquiring tough guys Jim McKenzie and Stu Grimson during the offseason.

Kelly Chase is undersized by heavyweight standards, but that hasn't stopped him from being a willing combatant throughout his career. Here he tangles with Sylvain Lefebvre.

Chicago Blackhawk Bobby Hull's battle with John Ferguson (center) is evidence of Ferguson's belief that no one was immune from his persecution. He was willing to go after any player, regardless of the player's standing in the game, if he felt it would help his team win. *(Photo courtesy of John Ferguson)*

All enforcers understand the unwritten rules of engagement. "If I take a run at Detroit's Steve Yzerman, I know I will have to deal with Joey Kocur," Chase says. Kocur is known as one of the top punchers in hockey history. It's widely accepted that the Red Wings' signing of Kocur as a free agent on December 27, 1996, played a key role in helping Detroit win back-to-back titles. With Kocur in the lineup, Detroit's skilled players like Yzerman, Sergei Fedorov, Igor Larionov, and Nicklas Lidstrom operate without the fear of being treated in an overly rough way.

Flag Waver

When a team is uninspired or playing listlessly, the tough guy's job is to inspire them. If his team is two goals down, a tough guy will begin looking for the proper dance partner, who might not be the other team's toughest guy. Remember, his goal is to win the fight convincingly as a means of firing up his teammates. Given how many tough heavyweights now roam the league, the selection process becomes crucial.

"Who in the league now knows he can grab the other team's tough guy and win?" Chase asks. "If you are going to change the momentum, you might want to look at the guy who fights but isn't the heavyweight. You pick a guy you think you can handle. Maybe you do feel comfortable with the other team's heavyweight, but you have to be able to handle him."

Chase has had some experience with that philosophy from the other side. He's viewed as being as ferocious as a junkyard dog, but he weighs just 193 pounds. His two tough guy teammates, Tony Twist and Rudy Poeschek, weigh in at 235 and 222, respectively. "When you look at our team before the game, I have a line of guys looking at me. If they are going to fight, I'm the one," Chase says. "I don't know how I ever got to be the heavyweight. That's how it is in training camp. These young guys come in and all Twister has to do is walk through the weight room, and they look at him say: 'Not a chance.' I'm never in the weight room, but if I was, those guys would say: 'There's the guy I'm fighting.'"

Tough guys try not to initiate a scrap while their team is leading because they don't want to risk allowing the other team a power play opportunity. "All I ever say to my teams is if you are ahead by a goal or two, no fighting allowed," says Florida general manager Bryan Murray. "If you are behind a goal or two, you are allowed the fight as a necessity."

Nick Kypreos (left) tries to grab a piece of Chris Simon's jersey just before Simon connects with an overhand left.

Personal Feud

Some guys square off simply because they have bad history with each other, though it doesn't happen as much as it once did. The changing nature of the game has reduced the number of personal feud scraps. These fights usually occur when a game's score is lopsided, and few games are lopsided these days now that defense rules. "I don't think there is as much personal animosity as people would speculate about players with that specific role," Grimson says. "Guys for the most part treat it as a business. I see guys after the game. I'm not saying there is anything superficial or artificial about the fights, but guys leave it on the ice."

Philip Crowe, then with Los Angeles, and Darren McCarty (right) lock arms in the classic pose of a NHL fight. One of the basic strategies of a hockey fight is to pull the opponent's jersey over his arms and head and then fire away with punches.

The New York Rangers' John MacLean drags down an official who had ventured in close because he thought hostilities were about to break out between MacLean and the Philadelphia player.

Mutual Destruction

Teams load up on tough guys for the same reason the United States and the Soviet Union ringed their respective countries with long-range missiles. Deterrence is a major part of the fighting. "If fighting wasn't in the game, there would be a lot more injuries," says Toronto winger Tie Domi. "You take care of all your teammates, but you especially take care of the elite players. The league knows how important we are because fans don't want to see the elite guys out of the lineup."

In order to win their second consecutive Stanley Cup championship in 1997-98, the Red Wings had one proven fighter on every line. Brendan Shanahan, Darren McCarty, Martin Lapointe, and Joe Kocur all play on different lines, and Kocur and McCarty are the heavyweight contenders. "The Detroit Red Wings don't have many fights because they have the nuclear weapons," says Nashville general manager David Poile.

Fighting is so ingrained in hockey's history that officiating a hockey fight is almost an art form in itself. While the referee is required to stand in the background and pass judgment on penalty infractions, the linesmen bear the responsibility of breaking up fights. They deserve hazard pay for such a role. Through the years, linesmen have suffered broken jaws, butchered hands, and mangled knees while trying to maintain order in a hockey fight. The NHL schools linesmen on how to deal with fights. The league's advice in capsule form is if you can stop a fight before it starts, do so. If you can't without putting yourself in jeopardy or risking giving one combatant a temporary advantage, then get out of the way and let them scrap.

At that point, linesmen begin to look for the proper time to separate two fighters. This is when experience becomes crucial. "We have to provide for the safety of the player," says Lewis, now the NHL's Director of Officiating. "The cute thing is sometimes you have a player who is sending you the message: 'Get in quick. I don't want to go. Help me stop it.' You have that component. Then you have the other guy saying, 'Why don't you stay out and let us go?' You can't win in your approach."

The best linesmen seem to sense when fighters have had enough. Usually fighters know when it's time to quit, and they send messages to linesmen with their body language. Linesmen look for signs that players are tiring, and they move in, one linesman tying up each combatant. It's at this point that linesmen sometimes become amateur psychologists. The fighters' adrenaline is still raging, and they need some assurance to get them calmed down and moving peacefully toward the penalty box.

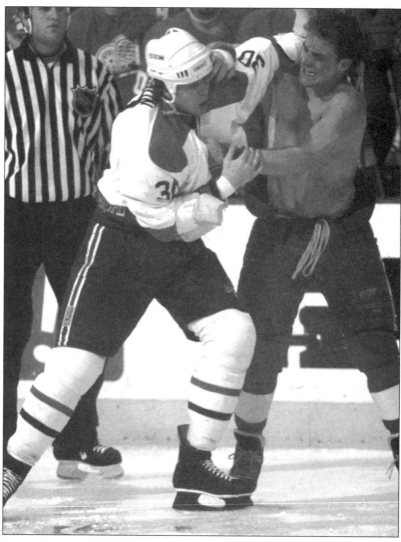

Darren McCarty, shown here after he lost his sweater and shoulder pads in a bout, might be losing his standing in the heavyweight community. He has played so often with future Hall of Famer Steve Yzerman and so well offensively that he's probably more of a power forward now than a tough guy. But most of the league's top players know that McCarty can fight with the best. He's capable of giving a whipping to anyone in the league, especially if one chooses to bother any of the players on his team. He plays with tremendous fire and emotion, and is always at the front of the line when a game turns ugly.

"All the guy wants to hear after a fight is that he's the champ," Lewis says. "One linesman will be telling the guy in green: 'Way to go, great fight. The other guy wanted to end it. You're the winner.' Meanwhile, the other linesman is telling the guy in white: 'Way to go, you beat the hell out of him.' Everyone goes away happy." Part of the tradition is that each fighter gets an "attaboy" from teammates. Players on the bench pound their sticks on the boards to salute their gladiator, much like the knights of old would have raised their swords to salute one of their triumphant brethren.

"A fighter wants to be told he's had a good fight, even if his nose is three inches from where it should be," Lewis says. "Blood may be dripping from him and he's delirious going to the bench, and guys will be telling him 'Way to go, you just pounded the guy.' And I (as the referee) would be telling him the same thing."

When it comes to fighting, there has always been a method even in the midst of the madness of the 1970s. Since the NHL's early years, coaches have used fighters to intimidate the opposition. The legendary Conn Smythe once authored the famous line: "If you can beat a team in the alley, you can beat them on the ice."

The fighter's role was viewed as an extremely important one. Consider that when Montreal's John Ferguson squared off against Ted Green in one 1960s playoff fight, many sensed the fight would decide the series. Ferguson ended up winning the battle and Montreal won the series. "But if Ferguson would have lost that fight, the series would have probably gone the other way," speculates St. Louis Blues vice president Ron Caron, a former scout for the Montreal organization.

One fight was said to have had a profound effect on the Detroit Red Wings' 1997 Stanley Cup run. Darren McCarty pulverized Colorado winger Claude Lemieux during a wild melee that also included goaltender Mike Vernon pounding on Avalanche goaltender Patrick Roy.

"They won the Cup that night," Roy would say later.

McCarty's fight with Lemieux, which left the latter bloodied along the boards, was in retaliation for Lemieux's nasty check against McCarty's teammate and close friend, Kris Draper, during the 1996 playoffs. Draper's face was so badly damaged that plastic surgery was required. Even though revenge was McCarty's motive, the fight seemed to unify the Red Wings and demoralize the Avalanche, the defending Stanley Cup champions. Suddenly, Colorado Avalanche general manager Pierre Lacroix was under fire for trading away tough guy Chris Simon. In the playoffs, the Avalanche weren't the same team they were the season before.

The days when fights determine a playoff series are long since over. Rarely do you see fights in the playoffs because the consequence of drawing an extra penalty is just too severe. Although many fight fans consider Tony Twist the league's toughest fighter, the Blues didn't use him in the 1998 playoffs. "Tough guys now have to be able to play," says Los Angeles Kings defenseman Rob Blake. "That's why guys like Marty McSorley, Bob Probert, and Chris Simon are so valuable, and a guy like Tie Domi. Tie Domi is a very effective player down low."

Kings general manager Dave Taylor says it was L.A. coach Larry Robinson who best summarized the enforcer strategy embraced by most teams in the 1990s. "If we just want a guy to fight we will go to the penitentiary and find one," Robinson said. "We need a guy who can play."

With that in mind, the Kings are very patient with 6-foot-6 heavyweight Matt Johnson, considered by many to be one of the rising stars in the heavyweight class. In 1997-98, he was playing about six minutes per game as the Kings waited for his hockey skills to catch up with his punching ability. "People don't want to fight him," Blake says. "Some will, but there is a real respect for him on the ice. When he is in the game, the game is much more calm."

One belief of veterans around the league is that high-sticking and cheap shots would be reduced significantly if heavyweights were allowed to impose vigilante justice. A few minutes spent fighting Marty McSorley could certainly convince a player to keep his stick down.

"Some general managers tell us to let the players solve this," Lewis says. "If Jones hits Smith over the head with the stick, let them take the law into their own hands. Our rulebook doesn't agree with that. But there is the law of the jungle which says when someone initiates something unfairly in a hockey game there is a bit of a payback that discreetly goes on all night."

Kelly Chase believes the player's code of ethics has changed in the 1990s. "Guys don't have as much respect for each other," he says. "There is a lot of shit that goes on behind the play, the dirty stuff, the hitting from behind, the slashing, the yapping. That used to get taken care of by the players themselves. There's always been agitators in the league, but there was always a point where they drew the line. Now that line has moved a lot farther to the extreme."

Everyone in the league understands that tough guys are handicapped. "The extra penalty is a big thing," Chase says. "You turn the other cheek now and you give your team the power play. In the past, guys wouldn't do that. Now everyone is a tough guy. They have something to say. They can hide behind the rules a little bit. Before, you just got your ass kicked when you acted like that."

Some NHL players, including Lady Byng Trophy winner Paul Kariya, have called for the league to eliminate the instigator rule so the tough guys can police the game themselves. Others say this would

If you held a boxing tournament to crown the NHL heavyweight champion, the heavy betting would probably be on Tony Twist. He owns a Mark McGwire-like upper body, plus a set of Popeye arms. The weight room is his second home. He comes by his boxing prowess and toughness honestly; his grandfather Harry Twist owned the welterweight title in Canada fighting under the name of Harry Runcorn, and his grandmother, Ethel, is in the British Columbia Lacrosse Hall of Fame. (She was nicknamed "Dirty Andy" in her heyday.) "Twister can punch— there's no doubt about that," says his teammate Kelly Chase. Twist likes to pound opponents quickly, figuring that's the best way to discourage "repeat customers."

The Los Angeles Kings' Matt Johnson gets his right hand free as he sets up to go toe-to-toe with Chicago's Jim Cummins.

make the NHL seem like the streets of Laredo, where the meanest, best-armed teams would rule. Because of the public relations nightmare that would follow, it's not likely that the NHL would embrace the idea of eliminating the instigator rule. Still, the NHL isn't looking to legislate fighting out of the game, preferring to let natural evolution take its course. Fighting is down significantly from its peak period in 1987-88, when there was an average of 1.07 fights per game, according to research by *The Hockey News*. In 1998-99, there were about .620 fights per game. Will teams disarm on their own? "It's like having nuclear weapons," says NHL Director of Hockey Operations Colin Campbell. "They say: 'I'll get rid of mine if you get rid of yours. OK, you go first. No, you go first.'"

Chase says a small, veteran group of NHL linesmen will keep the agitators in line. They'll make it clear that they'll unshackle the heavyweights if the agitators continue to run their mouths or push and shove after the play. "He'll say, 'All right, number thirty-nine and number twenty-two are going to fight,' and all of a sudden number thirty-nine or number twenty-two will say: 'Wait a minute, that's not what I wanted.' Then there is no more yapping," Chase says. "But the way it is now, (agitators) like (Detroit's) Kris Draper and Kirk Maltby have three Joey Kocurs looking after them because the linesmen always move in to bring things up."

Being an NHL tough guy is a high-stress, high-pressure occupation which subjects players to a high incidence of injuries. Every fighter continuously replays the 1995 videotape of Tony Twist breaking Buffalo enforcer Rob Ray's orbital bone with a punch that seemed to implode Ray's face. Joe Kocur has had five different hand surgeries in his career as a result of all the knockouts he has recorded. Fighters now fight approximately twenty fights per year, or once every four games. When they start swinging, their punches are just as likely

Noted tough guy Marty McSorley squares off to fight against Steve McKenna. One of McSorley's duties in his days with Edmonton and Los Angeles was making sure no opponent took advantage of Wayne Gretzky.

to land on the opponent's helmet as his flesh. "I've seen hands that made me think, 'If he doesn't have arthritis in them when he's finished, I'll be surprised,'" Lewis says. "You look at some of those hands, and you wonder what meat grinder they got them caught in."

In recent years, Florida's Paul Laus has shown the most enthusiasm for hockey fights, leading the league with thirty-nine in 1996-97. "He would have had more if we wouldn't have stopped him a few times because we needed him on the ice," says his former coach Doug MacLean.

More established fighters like Twist, Probert, McCarty, and Domi don't fight as often, although like top gunfighters in the old west, there are always youngsters who come into town every once in a while looking to earn a reputation in a hurry. "Once you've been doing it a long time, you get respect, and guys don't challenge you any more," Domi says. "That's why I end up starting most of my fights." Top heavyweights don't involve themselves in a debate about which among them deserves the heavyweight belt. "There really isn't a toughest fighter in the league," Domi insists. "There are a dozen guys out there that can beat you any given night. All it takes is one punch."

No matter where a fighter sits in the unofficial rankings, he is subject to bouts that could turn ugly before he realizes he's in trouble. Kelly Chase remembers one fight with former NHL player Link Gaetz that began as a sparring match and escalated into a nuclear exchange. "He beat the hell out of me," says Chase, who doesn't lose many fights. "I thought I was in a war with him, but then I got drilled. I kept getting hit. I couldn't regroup and hit him. I was just reeling for what seemed like two minutes. But it was probably twenty seconds."

As primal as hockey fights may seem, combatants share a fraternal bond that can't be appreciated by those outside their group. Tough guys are respectful of rivals' injuries, and more than one fighter has backed off when he realized he was trying to scrap with a wounded man. Tough guys routinely are known as the team's friendliest players. Younger enforcers who enter the league are somewhat surprised to discover that most tough guys don't hate each other.

Even in the midst of a heated scrap, some of the toughest players maintain their sense of humor. After one scrap, Stu Grimson and Jim McKenzie were in close quarters when Grimson started sniffing the air like he had just zeroed in on a pungent odor. "Did you have a little Caesar salad for lunch, Jimmy?" Grimson asked almost politely. McKenzie turned red. "Sorry," he said, laughing. "My wife's Italian."

It was Bob Probert who actually showed a young Grimson that when you leave the ice, the feud is over. Detroit was playing

Toronto Maple Leafs winger Tie Domi is known as a player who can yap as well as he can fight.

Grimson's Chicago team in the 1992 playoffs, and Probert and Grimson were bitter rivals on the ice. On an off-day, Grimson and his wife were eating at a diner in Chicago when he heard a loud, booming voice yell, "Hey, Stu. Hey, Stu." Much to Grimson's surprise, the voice belonged to Probert. "The nature of the Chicago-Detroit relationship was such that I wasn't about to wave at him," Grimson says. "I was new to the concept of relationships between fighters. I wondered what to do at that point. Do I shake his hand or grab him by the scruff of the neck?" But Probert chatted amicably with him like they were neighbors or old college chums catching up on good times. Probie didn't seem to care that the next night he and Grimson might be exchanging left jabs and overhand rights.

Making the tough guy role even more interesting is that often players move from team to team, which means that good friends could become possible adversaries. Grimson has played with five different teams, and is currently on his second tour of duty with the Mighty Ducks. While he was with the Whalers, he and Kelly Chase became close friends.

Now, the prospect of being back in the same conference with his buddy, but on a different team, isn't appealing.

"I never try to look from an emotional and sentimental standpoint," Grimson says, chuckling. "The last thing I want to do is fight Kelly, but you know what—you strap on the skates and put on your helmet, your adrenaline is running. If Kelly runs at Paul Kariya or Teemu Selanne, something will snap inside me and things will take off from there."

DAVE SCHULTZ STORY

Dave "The Hammer" Schultz swears he didn't grow up aspiring to become one of the most menacing villains in National Hockey League history.

"I was the quietest, shyest kid growing up," Schultz says. "I went to church and Sunday school. Everybody thinks I'm tough, but I wasn't. Why did I play so tough? I had to play my role. It wasn't something I liked to do, but I was pretty good at it."

He was actually masterful at playing the tough guy—never at a loss for knowing what to do to keep the opponent wary of his presence. He spun through the league like a Tasmanian devil in 1974-75, when he established an NHL record of 472 penalty minutes in one season. That's almost eight hours spent in the sin bin.

"He knew his job as well as anyone in the league," says his former Philadelphia teammate Bill Clement. "He would seek out the other team's tough guy at the start of the game and establish that he was the king of the hill. When he wanted to be in the ring, he was the best."

Intimidation aside, how did Schultz rate as an actual fighter? "When he threw a punch, it was like TNT," Clement says.

Lost in the flurry of Schultz's punches are the other contributions Schultz made to the Flyers' back-to-back championships in 1974 and 1975. He posted 20 goals—including 2 hat tricks—in 1973-74 to go along with his 348 penalty minutes. Twenty-five years later, Schultz is now an emotional coach and general manager for the Mohawk Valley Prowlers in the United Hockey League. "I know coaches do, but I cannot tell my guys to fight," says Schultz. "I'd rather they win with solid offense and defense than to goon it up."

He obliges the many fans who want him to sign old photos and memorabilia from his fighting heyday, although he isn't sure they truly understand what he's about. "What you envisioned of the Dave Schultz that played with the Flyers was a made-up thing," he says. "It wasn't me. I didn't like to fight. I've never had a street fight in my life."

Clement says that's true in many respects. "He was absolutely a Dr. Jekyll and Mr. Hyde. He never fought in junior hockey." But Clement says Schultz relished his Flyers role as much as Reggie Leach liked scoring the goals and Bernie Parent liked stopping the puck.

"He loved the notoriety fighting brought him," Clement says.

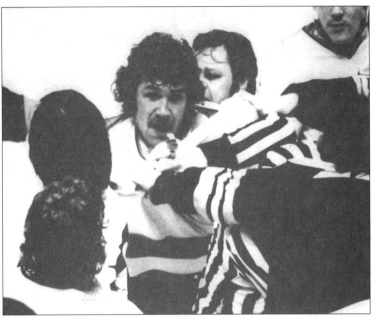

Dave Schultz had to be restrained during a melee against the Boston Bruins in 1974. NHL president Clarence Campbell threatened to suspend Schultz after he had 348 penalty minutes in 1973-74. He posted 472 the following season.

Anatomy of a Murderous Season

Here's the breakdown of the season in which Dave Schultz set the NHL record of 472 penalty minutes:

Minor penalties	61 for 122 minutes
Fighting majors	26 for 130 minutes
Misconducts	22 for 220 minutes

Highest single game: two minors, two majors for fighting, one ten-minute misconduct, and one thirty-four-minute game misconduct on October 25, 1974.

NHL RAP SHEETS

Penalty Minute Kings

Here's how the tough guys ranked in the NHL's all-time penalty minute list going into the 1998-99 season.

RANK	NAME	TEAMS	SEASONS	GAMES	CAREER PENALTY MINUTES
1	Dave "Tiger" Williams	TOR, VAN, DET, LA	14	962	3,966
2	Dale Hunter	QUE, WASH, COL	19	1,407	3,565
3	Marty McSorley	PIT, EDM, LA, NYR, SJ	16	934	3,319
4	Tim Hunter	CAL, QUE, VAN, SJ	16	815	3,146
5	Chris Nilan	MNT, NYR, BOS	13	688	3,043
6	Bob Probert	DET, CHI	13	726	2,907
7	Rick Tocchet	PHI, PIT, LA, BOS, WASH, PNX	15	990	2,773
8	Pat Verbeek	NJ, HART, NYR, DLS	17	1,225	2,665
9	Craig Berube	PHI, TOR, CAL, WASH	13	796	2,651
10	Dave Manson	CHI, EDM, WIN, PNX, MTL	13	919	2,604

It's no coincidence that Williams, shown here getting ready to add to his record penalty minute total, wore No. 22, the same number that graced Ferguson's back in Montreal. "Tiger was like John Ferguson in one way," Neale says. "If he thought going after some guy was what he should do to enhance his team's chances of winning, he did it. He didn't care who it was."

He drew the attention of the Ontario attorney general when he conked Dennis Owchar in the head with a stick, but he was acquitted of all charges when the case came to trial. Williams said afterward what bothered him about the process was that it caused him to miss two games.

Williams was a street-smart, mouthy, arrogant player who often rubbed teammates the wrong way and simply petrified the opposition. Late in his career, he said about his reputation as a fighter: "I get in fights because I won't give an inch to anyone. If you do that once in this league, you're history. But there are dozens of guys a hundred times more loony than I am." He retired in 1987-88 holding the NHL record of 3,966 penalty minutes over 14 NHL seasons.

Most Frequent Bad Boys

Here's a ranking of the NHL penalty minute leaders through 1997-98, compared by minutes served per game.

RANK	NAME	TEAMS	GAMES	CAREER PENALTY MINUTES	AVG. MINUTES PER GAME
1	Tie Domi	TOR, NYR, WIN	458	2,458	5.37
2	Gino Odjick	VAN, NYI	480	2,291	4.77
3	Shane Churla	HART, CAL, MIN, DAL, LA, NYR	488	2,301	4.72
4	Chris Nilan	MNT, NYR, BOS	688	3,043	4.42
5	Kelly Chase	STL, HART, TOR	433	1,899	4.39
6	Dave "Hammer" Schultz	PHI, LA, PIT, BUF	535	2,294	4.29
7	Basil McRae	QUE, TOR, DET, MIN, TB, STL, CHI	576	2,457	4.27
8	Mike Peluso	CHI, OTT, NJ, STL, CAL	458	1,951	4.26
9	Dave "Tiger" Williams	TOR, VAN, DET, LA	962	3,966	4.12
10	Bob Probert	DET, CHI	726	2,907	4.00

Fighting Penalties in the 1990s

The NHL has seen a decrease in fighting since the beginning of this decade. Here is a look at how many fighting majors the referees were calling per season.

1990-91	1.80
1991-92	1.75
1992-93	1.25
1993-94	1.50
1994-95	1.60
1995-96	1.45
1996-97	1.65
1997-98	1.55
1998-99	1.18

Although he's learned to contribute with more than his fists, Tie Domi, shown here battling New York Rangers' Darren Langdon, hasn't forgotten what got him to the NHL. "I don't think anyone is tougher than Tie, pound per pound," says St. Louis tough guy Kelly Chase. "Tie is one of the best at knowing what his job is. He's a little warrior."

NHL'S SOUL MAN: STU GRIMSON

Don't ever believe that Anaheim Mighty Ducks tough guy Stu Grimson is without a prayer when he squares off in a bout against the National Hockey League's nastiest fighters.

In addition to being one of the league's most potent punchers, Grimson is a man of deep religious faith. One view of Grimson is that of a pious scripture reader, a peaceful family man whose Christian principles are more important to him than his earthly life. Another view of Grimson is that of a fierce warrior with a savage punch. Those who have invited Grimson's fist on the point of their jaw or have been bloodied by his combinations probably have difficulty viewing Grimson as a holy man. But he has never had difficulty reconciling his vocation as a hockey enforcer with his life as a born-again Christian.

"If there has to be a player in this team environment that sticks up for the smaller man or the less physical athlete, why wouldn't it be a Christian?" Grimson asks. "Why wouldn't it be a guy like me that rushes to someone else's aid?"

Grimson says that ever since his days growing up in Kamloops, British Columbia, he has always felt a calling to be his team's policeman.

"When someone gets taken advantage of out there, I've always viewed it as my responsibility to set things straight," he says.

Grimson began his NHL career with two brief call-ups with the Calgary Flames in 1988-89 and 1989-90. However, his reputation as a tough guy really didn't begin to grow until the Chicago Blackhawks claimed him on waivers in 1990. The 'Hawks hoped he could keep Bob Probert from reigning without dissent in the Chicago-Detroit rivalry. He fought toe-to-toe with Probert many times, and always managed to hold his own.

The birth of his devout Christian faith almost coincides with his arrival in pro hockey. He was born again in the summer of 1987, and the following winter the 6-foot-5, 227-pound Grimson drew attention as a rookie in the International Hockey League with 268 penalty minutes in just 38 games, an average of over 7 minutes per game. The following season, he amassed 397 penalty minutes in 72 games. It's been suggested to Grimson that he compartmentalizes his faith and his playing style, maintaining his balance by viewing them as two completely different facets of his life. But he really doesn't separate his faith from his job even when he's fighting.

"I've never seen it as a compromise of my faith," Grimson says. "If I had carried that over to my public life it would be different. For me all of this is in the context of a game. To me it's always been a very cut-and-dry issue. Either a Christian man can play a physical sport, or he can't. There are rules to govern those situations, and for me it's just a natural extension of who I am."

Grimson doesn't claim any particular church as his own, although he says he is more at home with biblically-founded services. He recalls no specific Bible passages that give guidance to his role as a hockey enforcer. However, he says he has discovered "a host of situations" within the Bible that have provided him with direction and purpose, particularly passages that suggest that Jesus Christ showed anger in the face of injustice.

"Jesus Christ was a man who was quick to be physical when he saw things out of line, or out of accordance with his father's will," Grimson says. "In one instance in particular, he walked through the temple, saw the money changers and people bartering for cloth. He walked through with a cat-o'-nine-tails and set things straight. He was very comfortable displaying anger. Where my role is concerned there are parallels, maybe not as biblically profound. But certainly Christ was one who rushed to the aid of the physically weak."

Grimson is a mild-mannered man, once a history major at the University of Manitoba. He is known for his quick wit and his team-oriented philosophy. He's the good neighbor who would be a welcome guest at anyone's barbecue. But the moment an opponent makes a heavy hit on one of his teammates, Grimson

is in his face like a henchman trying to collect on a bad debt. He's had some ugly bouts with Probert, and a lengthy, memorable fight with Dennis Vial when Vial was with the Detroit Red Wings. Grimson says his ministers through the years have supported the unusual mix of his career and his religion, although he has received letters from pastors he didn't know questioning his role in hockey.

"Usually it's from people who don't understand the game, or don't know me," Grimson says. "But I'll be the first to admit that in certain instances I've done the wrong thing. In my role, I have to make snap decisions, and when you act out of passion and emotion, you sometimes wish you could go back and change things. But Christian or non-Christian, we can all probably say that."

If anything, Grimson says, his faith has helped him deal with his life as a hockey tough guy. He's always been a gentle-souled person trying to cope, living in a violent world where tempers, swearing, and physical confrontations are far more common than prayer and Bible study.

"It's a very stressful, physical, emotional kind of role to play," Grimson says. "It has taken me a long time to get comfortable with that, and my faith has been a real asset. I've been called to a specific life and role as a husband, father, and professional athlete, and I don't heap a lot of pressure on myself in those roles. I have released that aspect to God."

CHAPTER SEVEN

Fight of the Century

BOB PROBERT VS JOHN FERGUSON

Debating the issue of the toughest fighter in NHL history is an exercise that could probably spawn brawls wilder than any we've seen on the ice.

Nothing stirs passions in hockey fight fans more than the argument over who is the toughest fighter. Some argue Montreal tough guy John Ferguson is the most wicked of them all, while others claim Bob Probert deserves the title. The NHL's all-time penalty minute leader Dave "Tiger" Williams would also get votes, and St. Louis Blues muscle man Tony Twist would draw support from modern fans. How many times have we heard Tie Domi described as the NHL's toughest player pound-per-pound? Lesser-known heavyweights like Bob "Battleship" Kelly (1973-74 to 1978-79) also have supporters, and there are some highly respected hockey fans who believe the late 195-pound Bob Gassoff (1973-74 to 1976-77) was the scariest street-style fighter they ever saw. Many swear by Dave Brown, and his former Philadelphia teammate Behn Wilson would also get votes. You could find support for many others, enough probably to fill up several chapters of this book. Debating this topic can be as interesting and as fruitless as trying to determine whether Jack Dempsey, Joe Louis, Muhammad Ali, or Mike Tyson was the toughest boxer of all time.

All we can agree on is that we will forever disagree. But one consensus we might be able to reach is that a fight between Ferguson

Although Probert doesn't fight as often as he used to, he is still considered to be the toughest player of this era. The most important fight that Probert won was his battle with drug and alcohol abuse. He seems to have moved well beyond his many scraps with the law. Even in the midst of his problems, his popularity in Detroit rivaled that of Steve Yzerman. Fans chanted, "Probie, Probie, Probie," when he finished pulverizing an opponent. What made Probert special was that he was able to score 29 goals one season and still play rough enough to get 398 penalty minutes. Some say the Probert-Link Gaetz fight or the Probert-Craig Coxe fights are the scariest bouts of the modern era. Probert has never minded trading punches. In fact, he seems to scrap more tenaciously once he has taken a few jabs to his face.

John Ferguson would be the first to admit that he was a predator during his reign as the NHL's toughest player. As this photo would suggest, he showed no mercy when he was competing on the ice.

(1963-1971) and Probert (1985-present), at their respective peaks, would have had the potential to be the most entertaining. They were similar players in several respects. First, both were punishing fighters. Second, they could scare the bejeezus out of their adversaries with their eyes and relentless, sometimes crazed punching style. Finally, they could contribute beyond their fists. Probert scored 29 goals in 1987-88 while leading the NHL with 398 penalty minutes, and Ferguson scored 145 goals in 8 seasons in an era when a 20-goal scorer was exalted.

At 6-foot-3, 225 pounds, Probert easily wins the tale of tape over the 5-foot-11, 200-pound Ferguson, who would have difficulty dealing with the pure size of Probert, who always seemed to get stronger as a fight progressed. Florida Panthers general manager Bryan Murray says Probert was the toughest man he ever coached. Probert lost some fights, to Troy Crowder and Tie Domi in particular, but he never suffered a serious whipping.

"I saw him lose three fights, but he always came back and beat him in the second fight," Murray says. "That's the one thing he did better than anyone. If you fought him, you knew he was coming after you again."

Domi raised his fists in the heavyweight title pose—showcasing an imaginary championship belt—after his victory over Probert. In their rematch at Madison Square Garden, Murray remembers that Probert connected on forty-eight punches and won by a unanimous decision. Probert was a devastating puncher, particularly when he felt he had something to prove. Early in his career, Probert's effectiveness as a player was undermined seriously by drug and alcohol abuse, plus the accompanying criminal entanglements. He was able to turn his life around later in his career. But how awesome would Probert have been had he been in peak condition early in his career?

"(Probert) is among the toughest I've ever faced," Domi says. "He will always be listed among the cream of the crop."

"He's a monster," says Blues enforcer Kelly Chase. "He's looking at you with his eyes rolling back like he's a shark. Now you know you woke him up."

Probert needed to take a few punches to get into the fight. He appeared to own an armor-plated psyche that couldn't be penetrated by pain. "He's a second-half fight winner," says *Hockey Night in Canada* television analyst Harry Neale. "It looks like he's losing. Then in the final twenty minutes he annihilates the guy."

Even though Probert lost fights, he possessed an air of invincibility. "I always got a sense he was totally without fear," says Stu Grimson, who had many brutal fights with Probert when Grimson played for Chicago and Probert for Detroit. "You never saw any emotion in his face when he came at you. You never got a read on him. You hit him, he was unfazed. He was so proficient with both hands."

Ferguson started his tough guy career twelve seconds into his first NHL game when he squared off against Ted Green. By his own admission, Ferguson was a ruthless athlete who approached every fight as if it were mortal combat. This was a guy who wouldn't socialize with opposing players in the offseason or golf in tournaments that included players from other teams. He wouldn't even eat in the same room with an opposing player, which he proved once by getting up and leaving a restaurant in the middle of his dinner when Toronto's Eddie Shack came through the door.

As a puncher, Ferguson wouldn't have been out of place in a group of pro boxers. When Ferguson caught an opponent flush, the victim most likely felt as if he had just been smacked by a brick. Ferguson prided himself on always getting in the first punch, and generally preferred to fight along the boards or in the corners where his opponent couldn't dance out of trouble.

Former St. Louis Blues defenseman Bob Plager remembers a typical fight with Ferguson, who was known for his relentless punching ability. "He had a little cut on his face, and the Boy Scouts had to be called to take out the knots in my head," Plager says.

Ferguson intimidated opponents. He was so driven to do whatever it took to help his team that he scared opponents. They worried that he had no boundaries, though that may be why some say Ferguson never lost a fight.

"John Ferguson had no conscience," Neale says. "Even some of the toughest players have had a conscience. They knew when they had gone too far, and they were sorry they did. Not John Ferguson. A lot of guys who fight like the fighting, but don't want to hurt anyone. Ferguson would hurt you."

Based on the fighting styles of the two heavyweights, here's how a fictional Probert-Ferguson fight call might go:

Probert and Ferguson collide along the boards. Ferguson's gloves come flying off. He hammers Probert with two quick rights to the face. He's got Probert's sweater in his hand. Now he nails Probert again. There's another heavy punch. Probert's got a small cut under his eye. Another haymaker catches Probert flush. Probert seems stunned by Ferguson's ferociousness. Probert is starting to fight back, but Ferguson keeps landing.

Now Probert connects with a right. There's a left. Here comes Probie's counterattack. Two more shots to Ferguson's nose. Blood trickles out. Probert is starting to land consistently. He's unleashed a flurry of shots to Ferguson's face. Ferguson seems to be trying to hang on. Both players look tired. Linesmen look to move in, but Ferguson yells he's not done. Ferguson's starting to rally. He lands with a right and then a left. They are furiously exchanging punches. There's no defense in this scrap. One punch right after another. This one is a classic. No quit in either player. Where are they getting the energy?

Probert's fists are now like pumping pistons. Ferguson is delivering heavy payloads. His face is already starting to

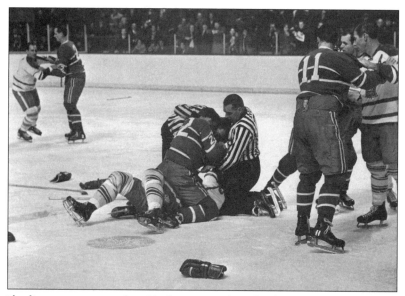

The linesmen come to the aid of Kent Douglas after he is pummeled by John Ferguson (top). *(Photo courtesy of John Ferguson)*

puff. Probert is showing several welts, and that might be another cut above his eye. There's blood on both men's faces. They won't be pretty in the morning. Probert's back is to the boards now and he stumbles as his skates hit the boards. He's struggling to regain his balance. He's vulnerable. Ferguson delivers two vicious jabs to his face. Probert grabs Ferguson's jersey and both fighters are hanging on. Their faces are four inches apart and neither seems ready to concede. The linesmen move in.

Those who remember seeing both fighters in their prime believe Ferguson could have been triumphant over Probert—at least in the first fight. Probert probably would win the rematch. If they fought best-of-seven? "I would have to give the edge to Ferguson," says St. Louis Blues vice president Ron Caron.

Ferguson's advantage? "I don't know if Bob Probert was mean enough. I don't know that he ever really wanted to hurt the guy," Neale says.

Despite his immense respect for Probert's incredible toughness, Murray also believes Probert's consistency as a fighter may not have measured up to Ferguson's. "Fergie had the emotion and fire all the time," Murray says. "Probie could be laid-back and passive, even in a fight. I have seen him not ready to fight."

A mean streak would be crucial to anyone wanting to survive a fight against Ferguson. Talk to the gentlemanly, cordial Ferguson today and it's difficult to believe that he once targeted Bobby Hull for extra abuse when Hull wore a football helmet to help him play with a broken jaw. Ferguson said he admired Hull's courage, but that hockey was not a sport that allowed players to receive special treatment. He was also the one on the bench in the Soviet Union in 1972 who suggested that Bob Clarke break Valeri Kharlamov's ankle.

"What the hell," Ferguson says. "I would have done it myself, if I had to."

Ferguson has a large amount of respect for Probert. In fact, he lists him among the toughest players he's ever seen. Does he believe he could have taken Probert? "I would have loved the challenge," he says, chuckling.

It is clear that fight fans are intrigued by a fictional Ferguson-Probert bout, just as boxing fans lament that it wasn't possible to see a Louis-Ali scrap.

"I would like to see a (Probert-Ferguson) bout," says Neale. "But I don't know if either would be there when it was over."

CHAPTER EIGHT

Men at War

PART 1: THE TOUGHEST MAN
IN NHL HISTORY — GLENN HALL

In an era when goaltenders believed masks were only for Halloween and equipment and pads were about as protective as a rolled-up Sunday newspaper, Glenn Hall's security came from his Kevlar-plated gumption and a bravado that seemed to be forged in titanium. After sorting through the eight decades of the NHL's most devilish competitors and roughest rogues, an argument could be made that Hall is the toughest son-of-a-gun ever to wear an NHL sweater.

This is a man who often said during his career that every game he played was "an hour of pure hell." Yet he was courageous enough to own the NHL record of 502 consecutive regular-season games played in goal from 1955-56 to 1962-63, which may be the safest record in professional sports. Pete Rose proved that someday someone would flirt with Joe DiMaggio's record fifty-six-game hitting streak. Someday a player will pass Hammering Hank Aaron's career home run record. Someday a PGA golfer will card a fifty-eight for eighteen holes. Someday a Hulk-sized running back will rush for 2,500 yards to shatter Eric Dickerson's NFL single-season rushing record. But no goaltender in the next millenium will ever come close to matching Hall's record, which he accomplished at a time when goalkeepers shunned facial protection.

To comprehend the magnitude of that accomplishment, consider that Jim Henry is the only other goaltender to play seventy or more

Chicago Blackhawks Hall of Famer Glenn Hall gets a mouthful of teammate Chico Maki's stick during a game against the New York Rangers in 1966. The player grimacing on the ice is Orland Kurtenbach, considered one of the toughest players of his era.

games in three consecutive seasons. He played every game in goal for the Boston Bruins from 1951-52 through 1953-54.

Nothing illustrates Hall's junkyard-dog toughness better than the night in Chicago Stadium when he suffered a gash on his knee that seemed as wide as the Rio Grande.

"Glenn used shorter pads then everyone else," former Blackhawks teammate Stan Mikita says. "There was an area between his hip pads and regular pads that had no protection. When he went down in the butterfly, it would expose the top of his knee and leg. In this game someone tried to jump over him and sliced him open with a skate." Mikita took one look at the bloody mess and presumed Hall was through for the night. "I don't know how deep the cut was, but you could have put your finger in it," Mikita remembers.

Maskless Glenn Hall (left) courageously played through injuries and his own fears to earn the honor of being considered one of the toughest competitors in pro sports history.

Fortunately for Hall, the injury occurred near the end of a period, and the referee ordered the ice to be resurfaced and the remaining time to be tacked onto the next period. He probably figured that would give the Blackhawks time to suit up the assistant trainer who was the team's practice goaltender. Even Mikita, who had watched Hall overcome numerous minor injuries to play, was amazed when Hall demanded to be sewn up so he could continue to play the game.

"It was one of the most outrageous acts of—you think I'm going to say courage—but I'm going to say one of the most outrageous acts of stupidity I've ever seen," says Mikita, laughing.

But Mikita is serious when he says that Hall had a will to play that was second to no one's. No offense to Baltimore Orioles infielder

Cal Ripken, but could he have piled up all those consecutive games if he had been forced to knock down screaming liners ten feet away from home plate? Granted, players are shooting the puck with far more zip these days than in Hall's era, but there were only six teams then. Hall was contending with Gordie Howe, Maurice "Rocket" Richard, and Bobby Hull on a regular basis during his streak. He was playing with Howe for the Detroit Red Wings when the streak began and with Hull for the Chicago Blackhawks when it ended because of a back injury. Hall believes that Hull could rip a slap shot harder than any player he's seen in any era.

"I've seen baseballs coming in at ninety miles per hour and always thought the puck came in a lot harder," Hall says. "I've seen (St. Louis defenseman) Al MacInnis shoot the puck a couple of times as hard as Hull. But he was the best."

Even though Hall would have only faced Hull's slap shot—which seemed to dip like a supersonic knuckleball when it rocketed off his curved stick—in practice, it's not difficult to understand why Hall's nerves would get the best of him, causing him to throw up before every game.

"(The vomiting) got worse later in my career," Hall says. "I found that I played better in those conditions. I didn't try to control or stop it. I encouraged it because I felt I was ready to play then."

Hall's pregame ritual was well known around the league. "We all knew he got sick before the game, and we were always hoping he would get sick during the game," says former NHL player Ted Hampson. "But it never happened."

Hall was known for not pulling his punch, even in practice. There was no question that Hull and Mikita used their curved sticks in part for goalie intimidation. "Practices were sheer terror," Hull's former Blackhawks teammate Al MacNeil told *Sports Illustrated* in a 1992 article. "Bobby had the hammer out all of the time, and he had no compunction about trying to put it right through a player's stomach."

In terms of self-preservation, it didn't help Hall that he played for a wide-open offensive team like the Blackhawks. Defense was never the Blackhawks' first priority in Hall's era. Hall doesn't recall, or chooses not to recall, many of his narrow escapes during the streak, although he does remember a Jim Pappin drive that caught him in the mouth and ripped open both his lips. About thirty-five to forty stitches were needed to close the wound, and Hall did spit out one tooth during the ordeal—the only tooth he lost during his career. He remembers the attending dentist telling him that given the severity of the wound, he had been fortunate that more teeth hadn't been knocked loose or out. He remembers that his face was so swollen, he had a hard time feeling "lucky."

Hall suffered his most gruesome wound when he was playing junior hockey, long before he got to the NHL. During a goalmouth scramble, Hall's right cheek was sliced open by a skate. The hole was so gaping that he could stick his tongue through the wound.

Hall wasn't just hanging on during his NHL streak; he was a member of the NHL's ruling class during that period. He won a Calder Trophy (rookie of the year) and a Vezina Trophy (top goaltender), and led the NHL in shutouts five times during the streak. In seven seasons of playing every minute of every game, Hall had forty-five shutouts. He never had a goals-against average over 2.97, and he made the first or second All-Star team six times. This feat is noteworthy simply because of the company Hall was keeping at the time: the goaltenders in that era included Terry Sawchuk, Johnny Bower, Jacques Plante, and Lorne "Gump" Worsley. All four would join Hall in the Hall of Fame.

Hall of Fame goaltender Terry Sawchuk, the winningest goaltender in NHL history, was known as one of the great warriors of the sport. He died of complications from injuries suffered in a fight with a teammate in 1970.

"There are always lots of very good goalies and a few great goalies," says NHL Hall of Fame goaltender Ken Dryden, now the Maple Leafs' president. "But there are very few important goalies. Glenn Hall is not only a great goaltender. He's an important one. He changed how goaltending is played. With the exception of Jacques Plante, I don't know if there is another important goalie in that way."

Plante made it acceptable for goaltenders to wear a mask. Hall's contribution was defying the conventional wisdom at the time by embracing a courageous playing style that put him more in harm's way. While most goalies today swear by the butterfly style, it's important to remember that Hall was considered both unique and foolish for playing a butterfly style in the 1950s and 1960s. Many of his contemporaries believe he was begging for a serious injury by playing so low in his crease.

"He was the first to really challenge the compromise of safety vs. effectiveness," Dryden says. "The way it was defined in hockey, as a goalie you played a stand-up style. It seemed like it was for effectiveness. Unspoken was that it was a safety compromise. It was a way of putting your head as far away from the puck as you could. You put it above the bar. Glenn Hall decided he would put his head below the bar sometimes."

Hall's style was born of a belief that it allowed him a quicker recovery time on rebounds. "He was always flipping and flopping," Mikita says. "He always used to say he wanted to make himself as big as he could."

In the butterfly, goaltenders play on their knees and then kick their legs parallel to the goal line to cover the lower regions of the net. "If the shot came in and it was low on the ice, I didn't feel strong enough to stop it," Hall explains. "If it hit the stick, it would still go in. With the knees behind the stick, it didn't go in."

Hall undersells the heroism of his accomplishment. "You could tough it out and play around injuries easier back then than you can today," Hall says. "We got shots from all over back then, but the velocity wasn't on them the way it is today. You could concentrate on the good players."

Through his seven seasons, Hall experienced a variety of medical problems, including the flu, contusions, stitches, and muscle pulls. His maskless face knew more than 250 stitches from hockey mishaps. He once had a reaction to penicillin after having a wisdom tooth pulled, and his eye swelled half shut. "They opened it far enough so I was able to play," Hall remembers.

As odd as this sounds today, Hall remembers that goaltenders in that era feared an eye injury, because it was potentially career ending. But they didn't fear facial injuries as much as they did knee injuries or broken bones. "Facial injuries just involved pain," Hall says. "It was just stitches. They didn't restrict your movements. You can forget about pain."

These days a goaltender wouldn't be asked to play under those conditions, even though today's goaltenders wear so much equipment that they appear to be encased in armor. They wear masks that contain a layer of fiberglass. "What's really stunning for anybody that puts together a long streak is avoiding the little stuff—the stuff that doesn't put you out for two months, but puts you out for a week or ten days," Ken Dryden says. "Those things just happen, they happen no matter how good you are or what kind of shape you are in. They happen."

Hall's mind was probably more important than his body during the streak. "Some (like Hall) don't make pain important," Dryden says. "They say it's there, but so is the rest of the game, so is the opponent, so is the importance of the game. You can put pain in a different perspective. When the game is over, then you feel the pain again because you don't have anything else to focus on."

One irony of Hall's streak is that it ended with an injury that did not occur while Hall was actually playing. He spent seven years in the combat zone, sometimes using his face to stop shots that seemed to have been launched from the mouth of a Howitzer. In the end, it was an act as innocent as tying a shoe that took him out of the lineup. He merely bent over to lace up a toe strap when he felt a debilitating pain in his back.

"You always felt you could play around it," Hall says. "When the adrenaline is flowing, you don't feel anything. I felt like, 'Hell, when you get into the game you won't notice.' But that wasn't true. I couldn't move." Wanting to play immediately, Hall sought a medical solution. He remembers a doctor requesting an inch-and-a-half-long needle and grinding it in his back.

"I remember crawling out of there saying: 'I'm cured. I'm cured.' I never went back again," Hall says, chuckling. "My injury was straight muscular, and it came around. I think I was out a week."

Hall didn't retire until he was thirty-nine, but the fear factor weighed heavily on his mind as he got older. Each year, he would ponder retirement, telling the team he wouldn't be at the next training camp because he had to "paint the barn."

The running joke was that Hall must have had a barn the size of the Taj Mahal because he spent so much time working on it.

The only thing that kept Hall in the game in his later years was the money, which he used to pay off the mortgage on his 475-acre farm in Stony Plain, Alberta.

"He really hated the game at the end," Bob Plager says. "He really did throw up. We would hear him go in the back room. Even though he might not have liked playing, he put everything he had into playing. He poured his heart into it. He loved being around the guys."

At the age of thirty-seven, Hall won the Conn Smythe Trophy as the playoff MVP, even though the Montreal Canadiens swept the St. Louis Blues in the playoffs.

"We didn't have videotapes available right away at that time, and I remember my brother (Barclay) and I thought we could have beaten the Canadiens, or won a few games from them," Player remembers. "We thought we had played well. Then the highlights finally came out, and Barclay and I watched them for the first time. We looked at each other, and said at the same time: 'We weren't that good.' It was the Glenn Hall Show that series. He was unbelievable."

After winning the Conn Smythe Trophy in 1968, Hall said he was serious this time: he was going to call it quits. Fellow goaltender Jacques Plante didn't believe it, telling reporters: "What's he going to do when the crops are in? That farming all summer is fine. But when the snow comes in Glenn will be pacing the floor. He will be back with us."

In October, Hall signed a two-year deal, lured in by a $47,500 salary. He finally retired two years later and still lives in Alberta.

Hall still does consulting occasionally for the Flames. He admits that he doesn't watch hockey as much as he used to because he doesn't like how hockey has evolved. The game doesn't live up to his personal warrior code.

"I'm boycotting the game to a degree. I get upset about it. I think the game has turned more violent than it has to be," Hall says. "What was boarding and charging isn't boarding and charging any more. They try to hurt you. It doesn't bother me much in the pros. They can look after themselves. But I have grandchildren playing and I don't enjoy watching the games because the games are so crude."

Surprisingly, Hall also believes that the NHL has gone too far in trying to protect netminders. "It absolutely bothers me the rules that are in the game," Hall says. "The goals that are disallowed—for the foot in the crease when it has no bearing on the goal—that really bothers me. I can see if the goalie is interfered with, but not when it has no bearing."

Lost in the enormity of Hall's incredible streak is the fact that he also played forty-nine playoff games during that span. Interestingly enough, the hockey world didn't pay much attention to Hall's streak until he played more than four hundred games in a row. "Streaks didn't mean much back then," Mikita says. "If that happened today, he would have five hundred reporters walking around looking at him to see what he had for breakfast."

According to Mikita, it was commonplace in the days of the Original Six for players to make a Herculean effort to stay in the lineup, but Hall took it to the extreme. "There was always someone in the American Hockey League to take your place," Mikita says. "I think everyone thought about that."

Hall did spend four years in the minors before 1952, when he landed a place with Detroit at the age of twenty-one. "In the minors, if you sat out a few games, you might lose your job," Hall says. "That's why you learned to play with pain."

PART 2: HOCKEY'S MOST RESPECTED
GENERAL — SCOTTY BOWMAN

The late Jean Bowman, a Scottish immigrant who understood the importance of job security, wasn't sure she wanted her son to grow up to be a hockey coach.

In 1956, Bowman was earning $3,600 a year working for the Sherwin-Williams paint company when the Montreal Canadiens offered him $3,800 to coach an Ottawa junior team. His mother didn't think it prudent for a twenty-three-year-old to give up a secure job to enter into such a risky profession. "My mother said, 'What will you do in the summer?'" he recalls.

Forty-three summers later, his temporary position has evolved into a permanent place among the top coaches in professional sports history, where he has earned the reputation of being one of the toughest coaches in any sport. The Detroit Red Wings head coach is hockey's George Patton, an accomplished leader who rules with a combination of intimidation, reputation, and genius. All that's missing is the riding crop and the pearl-handled revolvers. Bowman's many idiosyncrasies are difficult for players to understand. But players are clear about two facts: Bowman is always in charge, and he always knows what levers to pull to give his team its best shot at a championship. In addition to being tied with Toe Blake for the record of eight NHL championships, he's only one title behind legendary NBA coach Red Auerbach for the honor of being the major league coach with the most league titles. Joe McCarthy and Casey Stengel hold the pro baseball record of seven titles. Even legendary NFL coach George Halas only won six NFL titles.

"Without a doubt, Scotty Bowman is the most intelligent coach I've had. I learn from him every day," says Mark Howe, now a pro scout for Detroit after finishing his playing career with Bowman. "He's an enigma at times. Sometimes you don't know if he's half-crazy or where he's coming from. But he knows what he's doing. His knowledge of the game is second to none."

Bowman has never been timid about using benchings or other punishments to motivate players to a higher level of performance. His philosophy has always been that a coach should never cite underachievement as the reason for a team's failure. "If you have a fifty-goal scorer who only scores thirty goals, that's the coach's (fault)," Bowman says. "It's your job to get him scoring fifty goals."

In the early years, Bowman ruled his teams like a despot, allowing players to believe he would cut them if they didn't play to the best of their abilities. In the days of low player salaries and no-cut contracts, even the best players feared Bowman.

Former St. Louis Blues player Bob Plager, who played for Bowman in the late 1960s, remembers Bowman coming to a team dinner at Elroy Face's bar-restaurant in Pittsburgh and spying a jukebox. All eyes were on Bowman as he walked over to the jukebox and started glancing through the selections.

"Everyone is watching him because you knew he was going to pull something," Plager remembers.

Bowman pulled out a quarter, plunked it into the machine, and then stalked out of the room before the arm dropped the needle on the record. Bowman's message came through loud and clear as the song "Kansas City" blared out of the jukebox. The Blues' minor league team was in Kansas City, and the players didn't need to hear the words, "Going to Kansas City. Here I come," to know that Bowman was thinking about the minor league team.

One of the hallmarks of Bowman's success is his ability to stay one stride ahead of his players and opponents. One year in training camp, the Montreal Canadiens players said they couldn't run because they didn't bring their running shoes with them. The next day when they showed up to practice, Bowman had placed two hundred pairs of running shoes in the dressing room.

Montreal players remember that if they had played well the night before, Bowman would come into practice and explain a new complex drill in such a confusing fashion that no player could possibly decipher what he was supposed to do. When chaos ensued, Bowman would launch into a tirade about their poor attention spans. What players have learned through the years is that Bowman does everything for a reason, and that his motivational plan is so elaborate that he's often given credit for every odd thing that happens in the course of the season. When someone gets a parking ticket near the arena or the flight plan gets changed at the eleventh hour, everyone is convinced Bowman is involved. "Make no mistake about it," says Detroit general manager Ken Holland. "He's the general down in the locker room."

When Bowman was coaching in St. Louis, he wasn't happy with the team's performance. He called a 9 A.M. practice session, knowing the players would have to fight traffic to get there. After practice, he told everyone to stay late because there was going to be a meeting. The players waited in the dressing room until about 4 P.M., when Bowman told everyone to go home because he had changed his mind.

After the players had driven through traffic to get home, legend has it that Bowman called them to say: "How'd you like that drive home? That's what you will be doing if you have to go out and get a real job."

Bowman always makes his points with an exclamation point. His reputation for gruffness has made him the NHL's version of NFL Hall of Famer Vince Lombardi, though Detroit captain Steve Yzerman insists that despite his demeanor, Bowman's Detroit players "have grown fond of him" through their glory years.

In previous years with previous teams, the often demanding disciplinarian was not a well-liked coach. In Montreal he ruled his teams like a warden runs a prison. Instead of keeping inmates in line with threats of solitary confinement or reduced privileges, he commanded his players with threats of benchings and banishment to the minor leagues. The prevailing attitude among the Montreal Canadiens, first uttered by Steve Shutt, was that the players hated Bowman for "three hundred and sixty-four days, and then on the other day you got your Stanley Cup ring."

Plager has some fondness for Bowman, just as a former student remembers a teacher who brought out the best in him: "There are a lot of players who don't have good things to say about him, but I always got along with him. Say what you want about him, but I know that one day a year everyone likes him. When you got your playoff check, you said, 'Maybe he's not that bad of a guy.' "

Bowman's amazing postseason résumé reveals a league-record two hundred playoff coaching victories—seventy-seven more than those of his closest competitor, Al Arbour, who guided the New York Islanders to four Stanley Cup titles from 1980 to 1983. Bowman is also the only NHL coach to win Stanley Cup titles with three different teams (Montreal, Pittsburgh, and Detroit). Guy Chamberlin, who coached Canton, Cleveland, and Frankfort (PA) to National Football League titles in the 1920s, is the only other coach in the four major sports to own league titles with three different professional organizations. Bowman's aura is undeniable. "He might be the most recognized nonplayer in the history of hockey," Detroit general manager Ken Holland says.

One theory about Bowman is that he embraced a tough coaching style simply because it allowed him to win. Some say that if Bowman could have won in the 1970s by passing out lollipops and patting players on the back, he would have done so. Bowman's strength as a coach is his ability to adjust his team to make it more successful.

He still rubs people raw with a disposition as coarse as No. 2 sandpaper, but he truly has mellowed through the years. Plus, there are likable, quirky qualities to his personality that overshadow his edge for those close to him: the ties he wears for good luck in big games, the lucky comb he carries, and the passion he has for hockey card-collecting and classic cars. Those quirks just don't seem to fit a guy with a Lombardi-like my-way-or-the-highway coaching reputation.

Bowman is a very bright man with a lively sense of humor. Players say he cracks jokes, even during the last season in the middle of their playoff run. When the Red Wings acquired Ulf Samuelsson and his broken foot on March 23, 1999, it was Bowman who called to welcome him aboard. Bowman coached Samuelsson in Pittsburgh when the Penguins won their second Stanley Cup in 1992. According to Samuelsson, Bowman said: "You used to play hurt in Pittsburgh. Why aren't you playing hurt now?" Samuelsson appreciated the humor. "He caught me off guard," he says. "He's a good coach. When it comes to playoffs, he's incredibly good at adjusting to whatever situation occurs when everything is on the line."

When Red Wings winger Tomas Holmstrom switched his number from fifteen to ninety-six, Bowman asked him why. Holmstrom said he went with No. 96 because that's when he immigrated from Sweden. Bowman suggested that he should have gone with No. 98 because that's when Bowman would send him back. (Bowman denies the story, but players say it's true.)

Whether liked or not, Bowman has always been respected. He is a gifted storyteller, provided his audience doesn't mind side trips down three or four different alleys. He doesn't necessarily believe in finishing every sentence he starts.

"Trying to explain Scotty is like trying to explain abstract painting," said San Jose Sharks player Shawn Burr when he played for Bowman a few years ago.

Members of the media were surprised during the 1991 Stanley Cup Final when Bowman started to call Mario Lemieux the greatest player he ever coached. In the middle of a formal press conference, he began talking about how well Lemieux was playing. He began: "I've coached a lot of great players in my career. Mario Lemieux is . . ."

Tape recorders were clicked on as reporters anticipated the definitive quote on Mario Lemieux.

Sensing what was happening in the room, Bowman stopped mid-sentence and said: "Our power play has been really good in this series." Some reporters even began to laugh as Bowman spent forty-five seconds discussing the power play. He never returned to the topic of Lemieux.

Bowman's mind seems powered by a Pentium processor, which allows for the meteoric computation of facts, figures, and statistics. He revels in the minutiae of his business, and remembers facts from twenty years ago like they happened the day before yesterday. When asked what the biggest difference is in coaching players now vs. coaching players twenty years ago, he says: "They are making more money."

"I remember when the Blues took (defenseman) Al Arbour (in 1967), he was making about $11,000 and they wanted to pay him about $20,000, and he held out and got $81,000 for three years. I think he was going to retire if he didn't get it," he says. "Things really changed with the formation of the World Hockey Association in 1972. That was a big change. Players became more independent. For the first time, they had an option. Guy Lafleur was making $50,000 with Montreal, and the (WHA's) Quebec Nordiques offered him $450,000 for three years. Montreal came up with a plan to give him $1 million for three years."

There's no need to check those numbers, because Bowman is a man who thrives on details. He was analyzing schedule strengths long before computers were spitting them out. The number of practices per season, travel plans, and the number of television interviews players are giving are all-important facts to Bowman. One needs speed and mobility when interviewing him because it's likely he'll take you all over the hockey world. It's not uncommon for Bowman to take a question about the team's defensive breakdowns and turn his answer into a dissertation on the distinct correlation between winning and the combined percentages of both the penalty killing and power play units.

Many agree that Bowman moves off the main trail when answering questions because he only takes the direct route on questions he wants to answer. The minority theory is that his mind works more rapidly than his mouth, which is why those trying to interpret his responses are often confused.

Many members of the media have simply raised the white flag, giving up on the notion that they will ever understand his motives or thought processes. Other members of the media stay in the game, fascinated by this complex human being who truly does seem to enjoy keeping everyone on their toes.

"Everyone gets into Scotty's doghouse at one time or another," says former player Bob Rouse. "It's how you react that determines how well you survive under Bowman."

Bowman challenges players' egos to get them to perform. He knocks them down psychologically, expecting them to be stronger when they get up. He has always wanted his players to take out their anger at him on the opposition. Some say Bowman's plan is simply to unify his team by making himself the common enemy.

But he doesn't just use his amateur psychology on his own players. He is masterful at getting inside the heads of opposing players and coaches. "Scotty Bowman analyzes an opponent better than anyone," says Florida Panthers president Bill Torrey. "He knows how to prepare a team."

Bowman stills tinkers with his line combinations more than most NHL coaches, and he's never broken the habit of having a doghouse. He shrugs off the notion that he's more mellow than he used to be. He still doesn't socialize with his players. "(But) without saying a word, you know he respects you," Gordie Howe says.

When asked if he would do anything differently as a coach if given the chance, he responds in a surprising way: "When you are coaching players, you sometimes don't realize how great they really are," he says. "You never tell them how great they are. When I feel nostalgic, that's what I think about. I think about how great (Larry) Robinson was, or (Bob) Gainey, or Guy Lafleur, or Gilbert Perreault. And how I wasn't able to tell them how good they were."

Has he ever told a player how much he appreciated the player's ability? "Not really," he says. "You can't because it's your responsibility to get them to play better. If you have a great player, and he doesn't live up to his potential, those kinds of things disturb you."

Bowman almost quit in the summer of 1998, after his brother Jack died during heart surgery and Bowman had to undergo angioplasty to unclog an artery. In fact, Bowman told family members he was probably going to retire. But as his health improved, he knew he didn't want to retire. "What was I going to do if I retired?" he asked.

Coaching is his life. He was an analyst for CBC-TV's *Hockey Night in Canada* from 1987 to 1990, but jumped at the chance to return to the NHL as a consultant with the Pittsburgh Penguins. He then took over the team when the late Bob Johnson was diagnosed with cancer.

"What I missed the most was worrying about the next game. After I'd broadcast a game, I had an empty feeling. I wasn't used to that. I missed the competition. You could do other stuff, but it was an empty feeling because you couldn't cheer for a team. Maybe if you were with one team for eighty-two games, it would be different."

Bowman signed another contract to coach the Red Wings through the 1999-2000 season. He said one of his goals is to coach into his fifth decade, quoting the late Johnson to sum up where he is in his coaching profession: "He'd say, 'My coaching career is on the back nine. I just don't know what hole I'm on. But I'm out there somewhere.'"

One of the ironies of Bowman's Hall of Fame career is it was literally an accident that pushed him into coaching. He was a promising young junior player in the Canadiens' system, but his playing days ended forty-six years ago when his skull was fractured by a high stick from Jean-Guy Talbot. Talbot was suspended for one year, although later his penalty was cut to a couple of months. Doctors told Bowman he had to wear a helmet if he wanted to play. "And I wasn't the same player," Bowman says.

The Canadiens liked his mind as much as his physical skills. They paid his way to college and set him up as a coach, starting him with younger players. But even though he loved hockey, he shared some of his mother's concern about moving to Ottawa for a one-year contract.

Bowman took the advice of his boss at Sherwin-Williams, Bob Burrows, who persuaded him not to quit and to take a leave of absence in case he didn't enjoy coaching. "At Christmas, I called him and told him I wouldn't be back," Bowman remembers.

PART 3: THE NHL'S FIERCEST WARRIOR—CHRIS CHELIOS

The athletic traits that make Detroit Red Wings defenseman Chris Chelios the NHL's ultimate warrior are probably the same attributes military instructors admire in potential Green Berets.

"All I know is that if I have to get in a foxhole, I want Chris Chelios in there with me," Washington Capitals coach Ron Wilson once said.

Chelios has been dedicated to duty for as long as anyone in the hockey world can remember. The loyalty he shows to his teammates is like that of a sergeant to his squad. If you are on his team he will protect you, regardless of what he might think of you as a person. Even as a twenty-one-year-old Olympian in 1984, Chelios seemed battle-hardened. U.S. coach Lou Vairo was a strict disciplinarian who punished Chelios regularly. There were many days during the Olympic tour when Vairo wasn't Chelios's favorite person.

"But if I was walking outside in the parking lot and twenty guys jumped me, he would have been the first guy in there to help me," Vairo says.

Chelios is a modern-day Braveheart, complete with scars and mended bones. If he had been born in another era, Chelios could have been a member of the Roman Legion, a gladiator, a crusader, or a champion jouster. As a competitor who displays both an ample amount of ruthlessness as well as honorable gamesmanship, he would have made a splendid Black Knight. In today's league, he is known simply as the NHL's fiercest competitor. "He is the ultimate warrior," says Phoenix Coyotes winger Dallas Drake.

At 6-foot-1, 190 pounds, Chelios is a man of modest size and enormous reputation as an intimidating presence. To the opposition, he's a rogue and a merciless foe who seems to like hockey best when it's played more naughty than nice. He hails from Chicago's South Side, and his playing style was developed more from watching football than hockey.

"Every kid on the South Side grew up idolizing Dick Butkus," Chelios says. "I tried to play hockey the way Butkus played football."

Dick Butkus was an all-pro linebacker for the Chicago Bears who viciously controlled the middle of the field. Butkus reacted to running backs like they were petty thieves trying to invade his home; he took them out with prejudice. From early in Chelios's career, opponents were made painfully aware that they would have to pay a price to enter the offensive zone when Chelios was on patrol. "In one-on-one encounters, when he fights for the puck, Chris plays as if he is fighting for his child," says ESPN analyst Bill Clement.

Drake says Chelios plays the same way in every game. "He's not a big guy, but he's in your face the whole game. He cross-checks you, trips you—he's like the ultimate defensive weapon."

At eighteen, Chelios moved to Moose Jaw, Saskatchewan, to play junior hockey. He was a smallish, feisty center iceman, and it was in junior hockey that his playing style became radioactive.

"I was playing defense for the first time in my career and I was the only American in the league, so the whole league was taking runs at me and challenging me," Chelios remembers. "I had to learn to take care of myself if for no other reason than self-preservation. I had to become belligerent."

Vairo remembers seeing sixteen-year-old Chelios and noting that he was "a natural-born player." Although Chelios isn't viewed as a major offensive force, he has the skill and skating efficiency to play with the best offensive players in the world. He can quarterback a power play and jump into the play smoothly and effectively. But that's not what opponents remember about Chelios. They remember that he whacked their hands just as they were about to fire a shot on goal, or that he mugged them just as they were about to enter a prime scoring area.

Chelios went on to the University of Wisconsin, where he established himself as one of college hockey's premier pro prospects. Vairo's desire to have him on the U.S. Olympic team went beyond what he saw of Chelios on the ice.

"He always had a mischievous side," Vairo says.

At twenty-four, Chelios helped the Montreal Canadiens win the Stanley Cup with a playing style that sometimes bordered on criminal, earning ten points and forty-nine penalty minutes during the series. At twenty-seven, he won his first Norris Trophy, totaling 73 points in 80 games while piling up 185 penalty minutes. He never had to spend time polishing his halo. In the 1989 playoffs, he knocked then-Philadelphia forward Brian Propp unconscious with an elbow to the head, prompting Philadelphia goaltender Ron Hextall to charge out of the net for a wild melee.

Four years later, he set a Chicago Blackhawks record with fifty-one penalty minutes in one game. He totaled eight different penalties in that game, including a double game misconduct. He was suspended four games for seemingly pummeling Propp again without provocation, and for sucker punching Adam Burt. "He's just a lousy person," Propp told the *Toronto Star* at the time.

With all due respect to Propp's opinion, every general manager in the league covets Chris Chelios. Most of Chelios's allies agree, pointing out that his competitiveness sometimes clouds his judgment. That competitive zeal is legendary among friends, foes, and acquaintances.

Vairo used a game of Simon Says as a training exercise during the 1984 Olympic campaign. Two mistakes eliminated a player from the game. "When he got two he was infuriated that he got beat," Vairo remembers.

Chelios isn't a fighter in any sense of the word. He doesn't drop his gloves to square off against other players. "But he's not afraid of anyone," Vairo says. "He's got legitimate toughness."

In the 1996 playoffs, Chelios tore his groin muscle and then froze it before Game 4 to play against the Avalanche. Unfortunately, his leg was frozen so severely that he couldn't feel it. His teammates recall how tortured he was by his inability to play. It's that kind of competitiveness in which the hockey world exalts.

"When you talk about leading by example, this is the guy," says former Chicago Blackhawks goaltender Darren Pang, now an ESPN analyst. "He can go into the corner with a player 6-foot-4, 240 pounds, and come out with the puck every time. Then, he would throw an elbow just to let him know he won the battle. He also would gather the troops off the ice. There's some Pied Piper in him."

Chelios is one of the league's most durable players; he's rarely been hurt during his career. "His durability doesn't come from his equipment," says former defensive partner Gary Suter. "He just wears rags."

Chelios doesn't like his opponents to know that he likes to wear old-time equipment, which is light and lacks protection. He's essentially a knight who prefers to battle without armor.

In 1998, the first year NHL players were allowed to compete in the Olympics, Chelios was named captain of the U.S. Olympic team in another tribute to the respect he commands around the NHL.

On March 23, 1999, Chelios was traded by the Chicago Blackhawks to the Detroit Red Wings. The Blackhawks, thinking about the playoffs, decided to trade an aging, high-priced warrior for young, rising defenseman Anders Eriksson and two first-round draft picks. Chelios had played nine seasons for the Blackhawks and had told everyone who would listen that he didn't want to leave his beloved Chicago. It wasn't until the team declined his request for an extension beyond the next season that he agreed to be traded. He had been Chicago's captain; he owned a restaurant in Chicago. He loved everything about Chicago and won't say anything bad about the team, even though Chicago fans booed him when he played for Detroit in the season finale.

Chelios terrorized the Red Wings for years, but Detroit fans still gave him a thunderous ovation when he stepped onto the ice for the first time in a Detroit uniform.

"I heard some fans say: 'We forgive you,' Chelios says, laughing. "There were some pretty good lines (uttered) out there."

When Chelios's sticks were brought into the locker room, Detroit winger Darren McCarty joked that it was the closest he had come to a Chelios stick without it being broken over his head.

On the day the Red Wings acquired Chelios, they also brought in Wendel Clark and Ulf Samuelsson, two other war horses with reputations for playing on the edge. The Red Wings knew the roster changes were having an effect even before the first game. "(At the morning skate), everyone raised their level of play," says Detroit winger Doug Brown. "Legs were moving faster and passes were a little crisper."

Chelios's competitiveness was evident from the beginning. "When he goes to hunt someone down, he gets them," says defenseman Aaron Ward. "That has a catalyst effect."

Chelios is an instinctual defensive player whose judgments have always been of Hall of Fame caliber. He's such a warrior and a defensive icon that it's often overlooked that he's an impressive offensive player. He's a masterful handler of the puck on the power play and can trigger a fast break with a perfect pass.

Chelios himself always downplays his offensive skill, saying he doesn't view himself as a strong offensive player. "I find it easier to run someone down than to score a goal," he says.

But at the same time he insists: "I don't want a reputation as a thug."

Chris Chelios may be the best American-born player in NHL history. There are other candidates for that honor, including former NHL standouts Frank Brimsek and Joe Mullen. But neither has achieved the measure of respect afforded Chelios.

"There are other players out there who could be (the best)," says St. Louis Blues general manager Larry Pleau. "But since I've been involved with the league, he's the best."

THE FIRST SQUAD

Coaches are forever talking about players they would want on their side if they had to go to war. Chris Chelios is always among the first they put on the list. Here are some others you would want on Sergeant Chelios's squad:

Detroit's Ulf Samuelsson: Make him the corporal of this squad, having earned his stripes in many battles through the years. He's a battle-tested and fearless competitor.

Phoenix's Dallas Drake: Best open-ice hitter in the welterweight division. His playing style is feisty and tortures the opposition like bamboo under the finger-

The always aggressive NHL defenseman Ulf Samuelsson comes in high to rub out Dennis Vaske in the open ice.

nails. With his missing front teeth and wild-eyed relentlessness, he's got the right look for his style.

Buffalo's Vaclav Varada: Earned his place on this squad in the 1999 NHL playoffs when he was bullish along the wall and tough in some hand-to-hand combat with Ottawa forwards.

Carolina's Gary Roberts: Not the scorer he once was, but still has a playing style that is as prickly as a cactus.

Dallas' Richard Matvichuk: An intimidating force in front of the net who rocks opposing players with his hits.

Colorado's Adam Foote: Had to have his face stitched up after a playoff battle against Detroit. One of his favorite keepsakes is a picture of himself taken after this game—the stitches make him look like a war victim.

Richard Matvichuk (left) and Mike Modano put a sandwich hit on this unfortunate member of the Colorado Avalanche. Matvichuk is known for his rugged play in front of Dallas goaltender Ed Belfour.

LIST OF WARRIORS

It's always presumed that more fighting took place in the 1970s than in the 1990s, but tough guys are now fighting just as often or more often than the top heavyweights did in the 1970s. Here's a list of those who have led the league in fighting majors through the years: (GP—Games played; PIM—Penalties in minutes)

YEAR	NAME	TEAM	HGT./WGT.	GP	PIM	FIGHTS
1953-54	George Armstrong	Toronto	6-1/184	63	60	5
1954-55	Fernie Flaman	Boston	5-10/190	70	150	7
1955-56	Lou Fontinato	NY Rangers	6-1/195	70	202	4
1956-57	Fernie Flaman	Boston	5-10/190	68	108	6
1957-58	George Armstrong	Toronto	6-1/184	59	93	5
1958-59	Lou Fontinato	NY Rangers	6-1/195	64	149	4
	Ted Lindsay	Chicago	5-8/163	70	184	4
	Dick Duff	Montreal	5-9/166	69	73	4
1959-60	Marcel Bonin	Montreal	5-10/170	59	59	5
1960-61	Lou Fontinato	NY Rangers	6-1/195	53	100	5
	Bert Olmstead	Toronto	6-1/180	67	84	5
	Reggie Fleming	Chicago	5-8/170	66	145	5

Continued on next page

Denis Potvin (No. 2), shown here muscling an opponent off the puck, was extremely strong on his skates. Taking him on in a physical confrontation was like trying to battle a bull.

YEAR	NAME	TEAM	HGT./WGT.	GP	PIM	FIGHTS
1961-62	Ted Green	Boston	5-10/200	66	116	6
1962-63	Howie Young	Detroit	5-11/175	64	273	4
	Dave Balon	NY Rangers	5-10/180	70	72	4
1963-64	Terry Harper	Montreal	6-1/200	70	149	8
1964-65	Doug Barkley	Detroit	6-2/185	67	122	4
	John Ferguson	Montreal	5-11/190	69	156	4
	Vic Hadfield	NY Rangers	6-0/190	70	102	4
	Ted Green	Boston	5-10/200	70	156	4
	Reggie Fleming	Boston	5-8/170	67	136	4

Continued on next page

Paul Laus (left), shown battling Stu Grimson, is not usually listed as one of the top fighters in the league. But his noteworthy accomplishment of thirty-nine fights in one season (1996-97) could take years to occur again, especially now that more coaches frown upon giving up power play chances. "He would have had more that year if I didn't stop him a few times because I needed him," said his former Florida coach Doug MacLean. "He's a true heavyweight, he fights them all." The Panthers picked Laus in the 1993 expansion draft after he posted 427 penalty minutes for Cleveland in the International Hockey League in 1992-93.

YEAR	NAME	TEAM	HGT./WGT.	GP	PIM	FIGHTS
1965-66	Reggie Fleming	Boston/NY	5-8/170	34	42	5
	Vic Hadfield	NY Rangers	6-0/190	67	112	4
	Claude Larose	Montreal	6-0/180	64	67	5
1966-67	John Ferguson	Montreal	5-11/190	67	177	8
	Reggie Fleming	Chicago	5-8/170	61	146	8
1967-68	Ted Harris	Montreal	6-2/183	67	78	9
1968-69	Forbes Kennedy	Phil./Tor.	5-8/150	59	195	11
1969-70	Carol Vadnais	Oakland	6-1/185	76	212	12
1970-71	Dennis Hextall	California	5-11/175	78	217	21
1971-72	Keith Magnuson	Chicago	6-0/185	74	201	13
1972-73	Dave Schultz	Philadelphia	6-1/190	76	259	19
1973-74	Garry Howatt	NY Islanders	5-9/175	78	204	26
1974-75	Dave Schultz	Philadelphia	6-1/190	76	472	26
1975-76	Dave Williams	Toronto	5-11/195	78	299	25
1976-77	Dave Williams	Toronto	5-11/195	77	338	22
1977-78	Dave Schultz	LA/Pitt.	6-1/190	74	405	27
1978-79	Dave Williams	Toronto	5-11/195	77	298	20
1979-80	Terry O'Reilly	Boston	6-1/200	71	265	23
1980-81	Brian Sutter	St. Louis	5-11/173	78	232	26
1981-82	Bob McGill	Toronto	6-1/193	68	263	25
1982-83	Brian Sutter	St. Louis	5-11/173	79	254	20
1983-84	Chris Nilan	Montreal	6-0/205	76	338	30
1984-85	Chris Nilan	Montreal	6-0/205	77	358	28
1985-86	Joe Kocur	Detroit	6-0/205	59	377	36
1986-87	Wendel Clark	Toronto	5-11/194	80	271	29
1987-88	Jay Miller	Boston	6-2/210	78	304	34
1988-89	Basil McRae	Minnesota	6-2/210	78	365	28
1989-90	Alan May	Washington	6-1/200	77	339	32
1990-91	Mike Peluso	Chicago	6-4/225	53	320	26
1991-92	Mike Peluso	Chicago	6-4/225	63	408	34
1992-93	Warren Rychel	Los Angeles	6-0/205	70	314	29
1993-94	Marc Potvin	LA/Hartford	6-2/200	54	272	34
1994-95	Mike Peluso	Chicago	6-4/225	46	167	19
1995-96	Dennis Vial	Ottawa	6-1/220	64	276	30
1996-97	Paul Laus	Florida	6-1/212	77	313	39
1997-98	Krzysztof Oliwa	New Jersey	6-5/235	73	295	33
1998-99	Patrick Cote	Nashville	6 3/199	70	242	22

Trent Klatt's stitches and face discoloration are perfect examples of what players call playoff makeup. Tradition dictates that players ignore minor injuries to stay in the lineup during the playoffs.

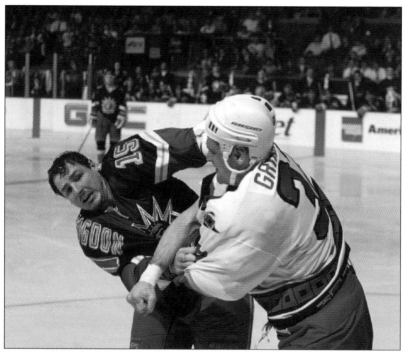

Stu Grimson, shown here as a Red Wing fighting New York's Darren Langdon, is a throwback to the 1950s-style enforcer who was referred to as "a policeman." Grimson is rather mild mannered until an opponent bothers one of his teammates. His pussycat then becomes a tiger. He has a heavy, stinging punch, although most opponents say Grimson lacks the killer instinct. Grimson probably understands his job as well as any heavyweight in hockey history. When a reporter asked him in 1998-99 about a couple of goals he had scored, Grimson said: "I never lose sight of the fact that the physical well-being of my teammates is my number one concern."

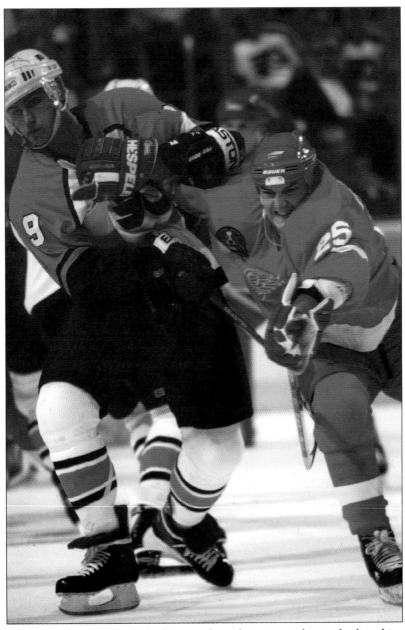

Detroit's Darren McCarty fights his way through Dainius Zubrus's check to drive into the Philadelphia zone.

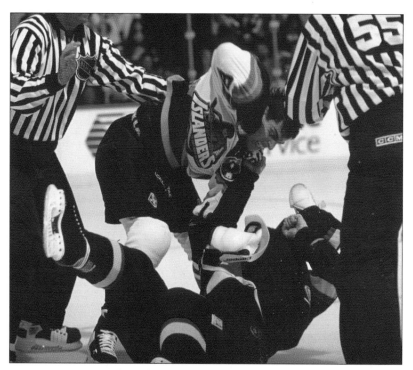

Marty McInnis, now with Anaheim, isn't known as a tough guy. But here he clearly has the upper hand against his sparring partner.

New Jersey's Mike Peluso emerged as the victor after this long scrap with Philadelphia's Dan Kordic. Peluso's fourth-line toughness played a significant role in New Jersey's 1994 Stanley Cup championship.

Jeremy Roenick is sent head over skates by this check from Winnipeg Jets' power forward Keith Tkachuk. The two players are now teammates on the Phoenix Coyotes.

Mouthy Esa Tikkanen, shown here battling Randy Burridge, is one of the league's most irritating competitors. His blend of agitation and pure skill has helped him win five Stanley Cup championship rings. He earned four playing with the Edmonton Oilers (1985, 1987, 1998, and 1990) and one with the New York Rangers (1994).

Mike Bossy, shown here getting tripped by Montreal's Ryan Walter, paid a price to score 573 goals in 10 seasons. "I played ten years in the NHL, and had a checker attached to my sweater for every game. We faced the checking line 95% of the time," Bossy says. He isn't sympathetic toward scorers who complain today about how the system has made it too difficult to score. "I hear about how there's more hooking, holding, and tighter checking," Bossy says. "I find that story so full of holes. It's as if we have found an excuse for less goals, and everyone is going along with it. I think it's a big crock."

CHAPTER NINE

Nothing a Leech Won't Cure

TOUGH GUY TRIVIA

Some of the NHL's toughest fighters and competitors are also among the league's most colorful and interesting characters. Here are some facts you might not have known:

• • •

During a brawl between the New York Rangers and the Toronto Maple Leafs in 1970-71, Rangers' rough-and-tumble winger Vic Hadfield grabbed Bernie Parent's mask and flung it into the stands. A few days later, the mask was sent back to Maple Leaf Gardens in a plain, brown box. No return address was included on the package.

• • •

Detroit Red Wings tough guy Darren McCarty sings in a rock band called Grinder, and journeyman tough guy Todd Ewen writes children's books.

• • •

Toronto Maple Leafs brawler Tie Domi once kicked a field goal for the Toronto Argonauts in a Canadian Football League exhibition game.

• • •

Howie Young, who earned a total of 273 penalty minutes in 1962-63, which was the NHL single-season record until 1970-71, was a part-time actor. One of his most significant roles was playing a U.S. soldier in the 1966 classic *None But the Brave,* starring Frank Sinatra. Young's character was killed in the movie.

• • •

In October of 1946, the Montreal Canadiens threatened to sign professional wrestler Yvon Robert to use against Toronto because they believed the Maple Leafs were clutching and grabbing too much. Toronto general manager Conn Smythe joked that if the Canadiens signed Robert he was going to sign the equally famous wrestler Whipper Billy Watson.

• • •

One good reason why opponents didn't like to tangle with Muzz Patrick when he played in the NHL before World War II was that he was a former Canadian heavyweight boxing champion.

• • •

NHL players are said to have recorded a "Gordie Howe hat trick" when they get a goal, an assist, and a fight in the same game.

• • •

Although it's never been proven, the media has reported that the impish neurosurgeon who repaired Boston defenseman Ted Green's fractured skull inscribed "Yea, Canadiens" on the plastic plate inserted into his head. (Montreal fans hated Green for his rough style of play.) Green flirted with death and was temporarily paralyzed when he was hit in the head by Wayne Maki's stick in 1969.

• • •

Eddie Johnston's courage as a maskless goaltender is unquestionable. In 1963-64, he played every minute of all seventy of the Boston Bruins' regular-season games. He was the last goalie to have perfect attendance in the regular season, which he accomplished by enduring four broken noses. "I broke it once Wednesday and played Friday," he remembers. "I broke it Saturday, got fixed up, and played Sunday." Twice, his eyes were swollen shut by shots. Doctors applied leeches to suck out the blood so he would be able to see to play. He played that whole season without a mask. "And no brains, either," he says.

• • •

In the Boston Garden's last season, 1994-95, Bruins president Harry Sinden announced that the home penalty box would go to famed Bruins tough guy Terry O'Reilly, and that the visiting box would go to John Ferguson, who terrorized the Bruins during a career that spanned from 1963 to 1971. Ferguson played his first NHL game in Boston, boasting two goals, one assist, and a very memorable stay in that penalty box after his first fight. "I sat in the thing twelve seconds into the game because I got into a fight with Teddy Green," Ferguson says. Unfortunately, Ferguson never received his box—someone swiped it before it could be shipped to him.

• • •

Philadelphia Flyers pugilist Dave Brown apparently didn't think much of the Lady Byng Trophy, noting once that he would only want to win it if they renamed it the "Man Byng."

• • •

Dave Hanson, who played the role of Jack Hanson in the movie *Slap Shot,* set the now-defunct World Hockey Association single-game record of forty-eight penalty minutes on February 5, 1978, in a game against the Indianapolis Racers.

• • •

In 1965-66, the Boston Bruins brought two junior teams—Oshawa and Niagara Falls—to Boston Garden for a game to show off their two premium prospects, Bobby Orr from Oshawa and Derek Sanderson of Niagara Falls. It certainly surprised many people when the two gems squared off in a fight. It was discovered later that the fight was premeditated on Sanderson's part. "My dad told me, the only two people they are going to remember from that game are Bobby Orr and the guy who fought him," Sanderson said. Sanderson and Orr would go on to win two Stanley Cup championships together in 1970 and 1972.

• • •

The Detroit Red Wings drafted noted scrappers Bob Probert (46th), Joe Kocur (91st), and Stu Grimson (193rd) in the same draft. Grimson didn't sign with Detroit and reentered the draft in 1985. The three combined for 797 penalty minutes in the 1990-91 season. Grimson had 183 for Chicago, while Kocur had 289 for both Detroit and the New York Rangers. Probert totaled 315 for Detroit that season.

• • •

Legendary brawler Dave Schultz holds the NHL record of 472 penalty minutes in one season, set in 1974-75 when he helped the Philadelphia Flyers dominate the NHL and win the Stanley Cup. In contrast, Val Fontaine played 13 NHL seasons and 820 NHL games and only managed a total of 26 penalty minutes. He had zero penalty minutes in five different NHL seasons. Schultz earned more time in the penalty box in one single playoff game than Fontaine earned in his whole career. On April 22, 1976, Schultz set an NHL record when he earned forty-two penalty minutes in a postseason encounter with Toronto.

• • •

Frank Boucher won the Lady Byng Trophy seven times in eight years from 1928 to 1935. His reputation as the NHL's most gentlemanly player was such that the league eventually gave him the original Lady Byng Trophy to keep. What's forgotten in the celebration of his benevolence is the fact that in Boucher's first game in a New York Rangers' uniform he fought the Montreal Maroons' Bill Phillips. Boucher had fight in his blood; his brother Bill was suspended two games for punching out a goal judge, and his other brother, George, retired in 1932 as the NHL's all-time penalty-minute leader.

• • •

Hall of Famer Tommy Dunderdale led the Pacific Coast League in both scoring and penalty minutes in 1919-20 in the pre-NHL days. Ted Lindsay and Nels Stewart were single-season NHL leaders in both penalty minutes and scoring during their careers, but did not lead in both in the same season. Lindsay led the NHL in scoring in 1949-50, and in penalty minutes in 1956-57 and 1958-59. Stewart led the NHL in scoring in 1925-26 and in penalty minutes in 1926-27.

• • •

The last fight in a NHL All-Star game was in 1955 when Detroit's Red Kelly squared off against Montreal's Bert Olmstead in the Montreal Forum. Kelly was a four-time Lady Byng Trophy winner, including 1953 and 1954. He didn't win it in 1955.

• • •

Those familiar with Wayne Gretzky's career insist that the hardest hit he ever experienced came from Toronto rookie Bill McCreary Jr. in 1980-81. McCreary crushed Gretzky with the hit. But it didn't do much for McCreary's career—he washed out of the NHL after just twelve games.

• • •

It was a near-tragic check delivered by Boston's Eddie Shore on Toronto's Irvine "Ace" Bailey on December 12, 1933, that led to the creation of the NHL All-Star game we know today. Bailey suffered a head injury so severe that he received last rites from a Catholic priest. He did recover, but his career was finished. The league held the All-Star game on February 14, 1934, and raised more than $23,000 for Bailey, who was able to attend the game and even shook hands with Shore in a ceremony before the game. What generally isn't known about the Shore-Bailey confrontation is that Toronto coach Conn Smythe decked a fan who screamed that Bailey was "a faker" as he was carried off the ice in a stretcher.

• • •

The Philadelphia Flyers' Broad Street Bullies of the mid-70s are often thought of as major league hockey's toughest team. But that honor might actually belong to the World Hockey Association's 1978-79 Birmingham Bulls, who broke the Flyers' penalty minute records. The

Bulls boasted such players as Steve Durbano, Dave Hanson, Gilles Bilodeau, and Frank (Seldom) Beaton, among others. Durbano won the WHA penalty-minute title with 284, followed by Beaton (279), Bilodeau (258), and Hanson (241). Opponents used to come down with what was called the "Birmingham Flu" when the Bulls were on the schedule. "Guys would sit out games, but we would spot them in the crowd and shoot pucks at them," Beaton says. "We broke the penalty minute record as a team. We had great depth. Nobody on the team had more than three hundred minutes. Everybody chipped in."

• • •

NHL referee Paul Stewart knows what it's like to be on the other side of the penalty call. Before becoming a referee, he was a noted hockey tough guy. While playing for the Cincinnati Stingers in 1978-79, he was tied for fourth in the league with 241 penalty minutes.

• • •

Hall of Fame player Red Horner of the Toronto Maple Leafs led the NHL in penalty minutes for eight consecutive seasons from 1932-33 until he retired after the 1939-40 season. The only other NHL player to lead a statistical category longer was Wayne Gretzky, who led the NHL in assists for twelve consecutive seasons from 1979-80 until 1991-92. Before Horner started his string of PIM titles, he finished third with 96 in 1931-32. In 1934-35, when Horner had 125 penalty minutes, no other player even reached 90.

• • •

Bobby Hull was no wallflower, but he once sat out a game in the World Hockey Association to protest the abuse Swedish linemates Ulf Nilsson and Anders Hedberg received when they were playing together on the Winnipeg Jets. To Hull, the now-defunct WHA was as lawless as the Wild West, particularly with regard to the use of sticks for intimidation. He began speaking out against unnecessary violence in the game, even though no one was bothering him. (If opponents had come after Hull, they would have found themselves chewing on his stick.) Much of the brutality Hedberg and Nilsson faced was a result of their European heritage. Ironically, by accepting the abuse, Hedberg and Nilsson helped future European players in the North American league. Their mental toughness (along with the toughness of the Toronto Maple Leafs' Borje Salming) paved the way for greater acceptance of European players.

• • •

The actors who played the famed Hanson brothers in the movie *Slap Shot* were actually professional hockey tough guys. The film was based loosely on the exploits of Jack, Jeff, and Steve Carlson from Virginia, Minnesota. A former Minnesota Fighting Saints coach remembers that when the trio came to WHA tryout camps in Minnesota "they terrorized every camp they were at." Not quite ready for the WHA, they ended up playing in Johnstown, where they became the inspiration for the movie. When it came time for director George Roy Hill to shoot the picture, Jack had been called up to the WHA. Jack was replaced in the movie by Dave Hanson, who went on to have a career as a tough guy in the WHA, and briefly in the NHL. All the Carlsons ended up having brief careers in major league hockey.

• • •

One of the funniest moments in WHA history occurred when Hall of Fame left winger Bobby Hull's hairpiece was yanked from his head during a game against the Birmingham Bulls. Hull and his hairpiece were inseparable; he wore it on and off the ice. But at one point in the game Hull went into the corner and came out bald. Years later, Bobby's son, Brett, remembered that it was Dave Hanson who ended up with Hull's rug in his mitt. Hull, by the way, was undaunted. He went into the dressing room, put on a helmet, and came out to net two goals in the game.

FIGHTING BROTHERS

After former NHL standout Lionel Conacher fought his brother Charlie in a game in the 1930s, no other brothers had a legitimate NHL fight against each other until Hartford's Keith Primeau fought his younger brother Wayne of the Buffalo Sabres in 1996-97.

Before the game, Buffalo teammates asked Wayne if he would fight his brother, and he shrugged it off, saying it wasn't going to happen. Imagine his surprise when he ended up hassling the goaltender in the Hartford crease, where he was suddenly confronted by his brother.

"He said: 'What do you want to do?' I said: 'Whatever,' and so we went," Wayne says.

Punches were thrown, although Wayne says they both were conscious of whom they were fighting.

"We didn't try to hurt each other," he says.

Who won the fight? "Probably him, but I'll say me," he says, chuckling.

Wayne Primeau says the fight went a long way in showing teammates how much he was willing to do to contribute. But he remembers that neither he nor his brother felt fulfilled by the experience.

"We were a little bit disappointed in what we did," he says. "But we also knew it was part of the game and it had to happen when it did."

Their mother, Peggy Primeau, didn't see it that way. "My dad (Mike) was laughing, but she was pretty upset. She didn't want to see that happen again," Wayne says.

CHAPTER TEN

Leaders Come with Iron Fists

CAPTAINS

Nowhere is it etched in stone how an NHL captain should behave, yet everyone understands there are commandments that must be obeyed.

Thou shalt covet thy neighbor's success. Thou shalt not kill, but thou shalt inflict pain if necessary to punish nonbelievers. Thou shalt honor the referee only because he might hurt your team's chances at crunch time. Thou shalt recognize that there is but one true goal—the Stanley Cup championship. Thou shalt not worship personal goals. Thou shalt not put anything before winning. Thou shalt perform miracles when required.

"By putting the 'C' on (his) jersey, we let everyone know who is in charge of each individual team," says Detroit Red Wings general manager Ken Holland. "There are certain things that only a captain is allowed to do, like talking to a referee. It's an important position, and coaches, players, and management take it as such."

Captains are expected to be as wise as Yoda and as dashing as Luke Skywalker. They have to know how to let the force be with them and that the dark side can make winning difficult.

No sport idolizes its captains like hockey does. NHL tradition demands that captains be held accountable for a team's successes and failures, an aspect of hockey that is not present in other major sports. In the hockey world, captains are well-known to fans. In Detroit, WJR radio broadcaster Ken Kal will simply say: "The captain brings the puck up ice," and listeners know he's speaking of Steve Yzerman.

The naming of a captain is considered major news in the hockey world. General managers and coaches spend countless hours worrying about the right and wrong time to bestow captaincy on a player. The Flyers agonized about whether or not they were giving the captaincy to Eric Lindros when he was too young. In Montreal, the Canadiens' captain may have more prestige than the city's mayor; he certainly faces more pressure. If the Canadiens aren't playing well he's expected to provide answers. The U.S. secretary of state may spend less time defending his or her country's foreign policy than the Canadiens' captain spends dissecting his team's performance.

"There's a lot that is expected of a captain, and when you take that role you know beforehand that there's going to be pressure, especially when the bad things happen," says Phoenix Coyotes captain Keith Tkachuk.

Even the rulebook honors the captain in hockey. Rule 14 states that "One captain shall be appointed by each team and he alone shall have the privilege of discussing with the referee any questions relating to interpretation of rules which may arise during the progress of the game."

The rule goes on to say that the "C" should be three inches high and must be placed in a "conspicuous" position on the front of a player's sweater.

What the NHL rulebook doesn't state, but what is clearly understood, is that the captain must have a hint of ruthlessness in his soul. He must set a standard for high pain tolerance and push the

When Philadelphia's Eric Lindros, left, and Phoenix's Keith Tkachuk collide, it is a battle of both strength and wills. Hockey tradition demands that captains be held accountable for the performance of their team. In addition to being their respective teams' best player, these two also are charged with inspiring their teammates to a higher level of performance.

envelope when it comes to punishing an opponent. Captains today suit up knowing the story about how Chicago captain Dirk Graham once played in a postseason game with a shattered kneecap. What would be considered dirty play or a cheap shot for some players would be considered heroic for a captain. He's expected to play with his sword waving overhead; he's expected to lay the lumber on an opponent.

There are times during a captain's career when that letter on his chest is both a curse and a blessing. One agony is that there are twenty-seven captains in the NHL, and only one ends the season stamped as a winner. As exalted as Yzerman is today as the longest continuous standing captain, he used to be blamed for the Red Wings' postseason failures.

"For years people said he wasn't a great leader," says Carolina captain Keith Primeau. "Then he wins two Stanley Cups and now they say he's a great leader. Truth is he always was a great leader."

No one understands that better than Keith Tkachuk, acknowledged as one of the league's premier players but still trying to prove he's worthy of the captain's bars.

"We haven't been able to get out of the first round for a long, long time, so that adds more pressure," Tkachuk says. "When people keep repeating, 'He hasn't won a round,' that's hard. That's a bad tag to have."

Although the expectations of the wearer of the "C" never change, captains accomplish their mission through a variety of styles.

Before Detroit captain Yzerman broke his record, Toronto's George Armstrong held the mark for the longest continuous run as a captain. He held the rank from 1957-58 to 1968-69. During his career, Armstrong twice led the NHL in fighting and was a skilled offensive player. He was never a superstar, just a very good player with natural ability. "He was a better player than we remember he was," says former Toronto general manager Jim Gregory, who coached Armstrong late in his career. "But he was a great captain. He was the type of player who management trusted and players liked."

As a former military man, Toronto owner Conn Smythe was particular about what he wanted from the man wearing a "C."

"It was like being in the military," remembers Pat Quinn, who came into the league during Armstrong's last season as captain. "Everyone had their place, their rank. But he was clearly the captain. He had a presence. He had a way of knowing what to do or say to whatever the problem was."

Opponents learned that Armstrong's outward demeanor didn't fully represent the competitiveness that always lurked beneath the surface.

"If he was smiling at you, you knew he was looking to cut your head off," says former NHL goaltender Eddie Johnston.

Armstrong was called "The Chief" because his mother was an Algonquin Indian. He was a big man, 6-foot-2 at a time when most of the players were under six feet tall. He had a commanding presence. Players liked him because he wasn't afraid of management—an important trait in that era. "If there was a problem with (coach) Punch Imlach, he would stand up to him," Quinn remembers.

One story former players tell about Armstrong involves the time Imlach told him to give a specific referee grief about a call during a game. Not wanting the referee to be mad at the Toronto team all season, Armstrong went over to the referee and started screaming at him.

To everyone in the arena—and to Imlach in particular—it looked as if Armstrong was berating the referee with a blue language tirade. But despite all the gesturing and screaming, Armstrong actually was yelling: "See the balding guy over there? He wants me to give you hell. But I'm over here to tell you you are doing one helluva job. You just keep up the good work and don't worry about the coach. I'll take care of him." Armstrong wrapped up his speech by shaking his fist at the ref, telling him one more time that he was doing a good job.

In the 1970s, Bob Clarke, from Flin Flon, Manitoba, led the Philadelphia Flyers like Attila led the Huns. He was a ruthless competitor who led his team with a flamboyant, aggressive playing style. Everyone who came near him did so with the knowledge that Clarke had once broken Valeri Kharlamov's ankle with a slash because he believed it would help Team Canada win the Summit Series in 1972.

Philadelphia's Bob Clarke, in the center of this melee, is considered one of the feistiest competitors in NHL history. His friends called him "ultra competitive." His enemies called him "dirty." He's remembered in Canada for breaking Valeri Kharlamov's ankle in the 1972 Summit Series.

The Flyers were willing to name Lindros captain at age twenty-one because they had watched Clarke handle the rank so superbly at age twenty-three. When Fred Shero named Clarke captain at such a young age, he told the media: "He's our best player. It doesn't matter how old you are if others are willing to listen to you."

As Captain Marvel on skates for fifteen NHL seasons, Clarke was a conscientiously hard worker with an unconscionable savageness when the game was on the line. His gap-toothed smile was almost the symbol of the Broad Street Bullies. Despised by fans in every other league city, Clarke was a demigod in Philadelphia, where fans understood that their back-to-back championships in 1974 and 1975 were won under his command. It was Clarke who had shown the Flyers how to win.

Having overcome diabetes to play in the NHL, Clarke had an aura of pride about him that seemed to overwhelm the Flyers almost from his first day in training camp.

"Clarke never came remotely close to taking a lazy stride," says former teammate Bill Clement. "He was the most driven athlete I've ever seen. He played with the determination of a man who thought his life depended on every shift."

Clarke won the Hart Trophy three times as the NHL's MVP. Around the league, he was despised and respected at the same time. Many opponents considered him a dirty player, but in the Philadelphia dressing room, he was the supreme commander. Clement remembers being in a whirlpool with a foot injury so severe that he couldn't walk, but when Clarke came over and said the team needed him to play, "you just knew you had to go out there and do it."

Clement remembers that in his early years, when his place in the lineup wasn't assured in every game, Clarke would skate up to him in the pregame warm-up and tell him how important it was that he have a good game. Clarke told Clement that he had asked the coaching staff to put Clement in the lineup. Maybe Clarke had said the same thing to other players as well, but it was all Clement needed to hear. "When Bobby Clarke says he (vouched) for you, you don't want to disappoint him," Clement says.

Clement is irritated by the suggestion propagated by former opponents that Clarke was unwilling to fight his own battles. It was certainly true that players like Dave Schultz and others made it their mission to protect Clarke. But Clement insists Clarke "would have fought to the death with anyone."

Clement likens Clarke's value to the Philadelphia squad to Robert E. Lee's value to the Confederate troops during the Civil War.

"From what I've read, Robert E. Lee wanted to lead his men into battle on several occasions, but he was so revered that his men would crowd around him and escort him back to the rear so he wouldn't be in the first line of fire," Clement says. "That's how it was with Bobby. He was our spiritual leader and we knew we couldn't afford to lose him."

No one on the bench ever said that Clarke was to be protected, but it came naturally to the Flyers' players. "It was an instinct," Clement says. "He would be in the middle of it and Dave Schultz would pull him back and say 'I'll take care of this, Bobby.' He was that important to us."

Boston Bruins general manager Harry Sinden described Clarke best in the mid-1980s when he told reporters: "No question he was a dirty player, but you could respect Clarke because he was so willing to take what he dished out. Look at his face. He didn't carve it up himself."

Clarke was uncomfortable when the Flyers hung his number sixteen from the rafters in a retirement ceremony on November 15, 1984. In a Clarke-ish moment, he indicated that the thought of having his number retired made him seem almost unworthy. "I always thought that was for the Howes and Richards. Me, I just played hard."

Bryan Trottier, who captained the New York Islanders to four consecutive Stanley Cups from 1980 to 1983, was also a member of the warrior tribe. He was a hard-nosed, belligerent leader with the skill to play a high-tempo, end-to-end offensive game and the strength and mental toughness to play hand-to-hand in the trenches.

"If you didn't take care of your defensive responsibilities, I knew I had a center who would have something to say about that," says Trottier's former linemate, Mike Bossy, who is considered to have one of the purest goal-scoring touches in NHL history.

Montreal Canadien Bob Gainey was also a respected captain, though he was a quiet man who led by doing his job better than anyone else on the team. He was like a World War I hero, a quiet, humble Sergeant York capable of surprisingly tough performances at opportune times. Gainey moved into the spotlight not because he longed to be there, but because he found himself in that role. That didn't make him any less of a leader than Clarke—just different.

Considered the league's best defensive forward, Gainey worked so hard in practice that teammates were embarrassed to give anything short of their best effort at all times.

"When I first came into the league, Bob Gainey was a god to me," says Dallas Stars player Brian Skrudland, a former captain of the Florida Panthers. "He was the epitome of what a captain should be. He wore it on his sleeve. You could tell when the team lost, he felt worse than anyone." Gainey earned five Stanley Cup rings during his playing career with Montreal, and no one was surprised when

Bob Gainey (No. 23) earned his captaincy with a hard-nosed playing style. He never had to say much to rally the Montreal Canadiens because most teammates would simply be too embarrassed to put out anything less than their best effort in his company.

he became a coach and a general manager after his playing career ended.

Vancouver Canucks captain Mark Messier, owner of six Stanley Cup rings, is considered one of the top captains in NHL history because he always knows how to command in the heat of battle. When the game is on the line, he seems to have the heart of a mobster and the combat skills of a Navy Seal. Those who have played against Messier never have any doubt that he is willing to push the outer limits of decency in the name of winning. He's one of the leading playoff scorers in NHL history and a sure Hall of Famer, and yet he has earned six suspensions for excessive violence, and probably deserved many more. Those who believe that superstars receive preferential treatment with regard to supplemental discipline point to Messier as their proof. You wouldn't need to look very hard to find those who believe Messier has gotten away with assaults through the years because he's one of the most respected captains in NHL history.

The Messier mystique may have been born during the Oilers' 1984 Stanley Cup Final championship run. He won the Conn Smythe trophy on the strength of eight goals and eighteen assists, but it could be argued that he cemented the trophy with his performance in Game 3. He was hard on the puck throughout the game, and sent the Oilers off and running to a 7-2 win with a flashy goal through three New York Islanders, including future Hall of Famer Denis Potvin. It was leadership personified, one man picking up the flag, rallying for a major charge. It wasn't Wayne Gretzky or Grant Fuhr or Paul Coffey who led the Oilers to their first Stanley Cup. It was clearly Messier.

"To me, it was Mark's greatest moment as a hockey player," says Bill Tuele, the Oilers' vice president of communications. "I don't know if this team knew it had the right stuff it takes to beat the Islanders until Mark decided it. That typified what Mark was about. He wasn't going to wait for something to happen. He was going to make it happen."

Messier has had many more opportunities to lead the charge. He's been on six Stanley Cup championship teams—five with the Edmonton Oilers (1984, 1985, 1987, 1988, and 1990) and one with the New York Rangers (1994).

Mark Messier (right) feels the butt-end of Bobby Holik's stick during this play-off series between the New York Rangers and the New Jersey Devils. When it comes to physical abuse, Mark Messier has given as much as he has received.

His most dramatic moment as a captain may have been in 1994, when he guaranteed and then delivered a victory against the New Jersey Devils in Game 6 of the Eastern Conference Final when the Rangers were down 3-2. In New York sports lore, Messier's "guarantee" is likened to Joe Namath's prediction of a win over the highly favored Baltimore Colts in Super Bowl III or a Babe Ruth call of a home run poke to center field.

It's said that Messier can also motivate through intimidation. Legend has it that Messier has bullied a teammate or two and has strongly suggested that a player improve his work habits or he would have to answer to Messier. The tale that has stood the test of time involves Messier allegedly pushing linemate Kent Nilsson up against a wall or picking him up as Messier berated him for what he considered a poor effort. Messier's motivational sessions with teammates are considered by many to be somewhat exaggerated. The players' code of silence regarding what goes on in the dressing room makes it difficult to separate the myth from the reality. But everyone is sure that Messier confronted Nilsson in some form, even if only to have a discussion about his level of play.

Despite his reputation, Messier may use benevolence as much as intimidation to get the most out of his players. "I hate to disappoint, but I really don't have any Knute Rockne speeches that I use," he says.

Messier also has been known to be his team's social director, and for going out of his way to make sure players, especially new ones, feel at home.

The history of NHL captaincy dates to 1909, when the Montreal Canadiens named Jack Laviolette as the official team captain. Since then, the roll call of captains also has been a list of future Hall of Famers. Fiery Ted Lindsay, Gordie Howe, Maurice "Rocket" Richard, Milt Schmidt, and George Armstrong were all captains during their heydays. "In the 1950s, the captain was expected to lead the team in scoring and win every fight," says Max McNab, who played briefly on a line with Howe and Lindsay before becoming a pro hockey executive.

As time progressed, NHL teams seemed more willing to give the "C" to players who weren't quite superstars, but had demonstrated the ability to lead off and on the ice. Montreal's Gainey was perhaps the best example of that type of captain.

Captains today also vary in style. Eric Lindros fires up his Flyers' team differently than Paul Kariya leads the Mighty Ducks of Anaheim. "I don't like to be rah, rah, rah in the dressing room," Kariya says.

"I try to lead by example. I think that's the best way. It doesn't matter what you say if you don't go out there and do it."

Yzerman also leads more by example, a style he developed as a youngster idolizing Bryan Trottier. "I liked the way he played. I liked the Islanders, and I tried to copy the way he played," Yzerman says. He has even copied Trottier's little jab, and will give it to opponents if they cross his line of how the game should be played.

Being a captain requires a player to be a blend of a

With two Stanley Cups now on his résumé, Detroit captain Steve Yzerman, shown here with blood streaming down his face, has earned a reputation as one of the league's fiercest warriors. Yzerman will give a hit, take a hit, block a shot, or do whatever else it takes to win.

father, a brother, a coach, and an amateur psychologist. "The captain's role in the locker room and away from the rink can be more important or just as important as his role on the ice," says Buffalo captain Mike Peca.

Many of today's captains wish they possessed Messier's iron fist, but understand that would work only for him. "I've heard the stories about how (Messier) was able to get in guys' faces and challenge them," Peca says. "Everyone has their own ways of going about things. Mark Messier commands so much respect he can do certain things. I've always been the type of guy who doesn't want to embarrass people in front of a crowd. I like to talk to people one-on-one. I try to make it positive."

It's a complicated formula, Peca insists, because every scenario requires a different reaction. "Dealing with all those situations can really mount on you sometimes," he says. "You hold meetings, and then sometimes meetings can have an adverse effect because you have too many. But you have to have them because you need to air out your dirty laundry and get on with life."

If someone isn't playing well, the coach may get the first shot at turning him around. But it's usually the captain who is brought in to consult, because theoretically he's closer to the player than the coach is. Depending on the experience of the captain, he is expected to size up the situation and make an effort to help the player resolve his problem.

With players now receiving multimillion dollar contracts, team executives seem to feel more obligated to appoint their best offensive player to the role of team captain as quickly as possible. Unsaid is the belief that the "C" is supposed to remind captains daily of the heavy responsibility they have to the team.

The trend of appointing the team's best offensive player to the role of captain has helped tear down the prejudice against Europeans serving as captains. No longer is it said that that Europeans can't be leaders because they don't understand the drive of the Stanley Cup as much as a North American does. In 1998-99, Sweden's Mats Sundin (Toronto), Czech Republic's Jaromir Jagr (Pittsburgh), and Russia's Alexei Yashin (Ottawa) all became captains.

This trio of captains is meaningful because it puts a final stamp of legitimacy on an idea that seemed foreign when the 1990s began—that Europeans covet a Stanley Cup as much as North Americans.

"I knew there would be more European captains as soon as I met Igor Larionov," says Vancouver general manager Brian Burke.

Larionov, who earned two Cup rings with the Detroit Red Wings, hasn't been a permanent captain in the NHL, yet he's been acknowledged as a leader almost from the moment he joined the NHL. The legend of Larionov risking his career, and perhaps his life, in the 1980s to embrace a "players' rights" stand against the totalitarian Soviet regime preceded his entry into the league.

Articulate and introspective, Larionov probably appreciates the symbolism of the three European captains more than anyone.

"(Captains are) supposed to embody all the great parts of an athlete," says Carolina coach Paul Maurice. "They're supposed to be fearless. They're supposed to rise to the challenge and the pressure and not bend. They're supposed to be tough mentally so they can survive the season."

Boston Bruins goalie Byron Dafoe offers that the structuring of hockey into three periods also feeds the need for a captain.

"Three times we all sit together in a room and prepare for twenty minutes of unbelievable intensity," he says. "And ninety-nine percent of the time, it's the captain in there doing the talking, getting the guys prepared for the next twenty minutes of work. Everyone and their dog can see that (captain) Ray Bourque is our leader on the ice, but players know he does so much more for us in the dressing room because of his talking and getting guys jazzed up."

Carolina Hurricanes captain Keith Primeau admits that a player doesn't appreciate the heaviness of the "C" until it is attached to his jersey.

"The onus is on the captain," Primeau says. "People are always watching to see how you react in certain situations, not just players, but management, fans, the media. There's no question there is more burden on your shoulders."

Even in the heat of battle, the NHL's most hardened war generals also must be skilled diplomats.

Given how subjective officiating can be, most captains agree that the trickiest aspect of their role is dealing with referees. Captains and their alternates are, according to league rules, the only players allowed to question referees. Sometimes that's like asking the snake and the mongoose to work out their differences.

"My approach to refs has changed since I've taken over the 'C,'" Primeau says. "I used to berate and taunt refs more before I was a captain. Now I tone it down because I feel I need them. If there's something borderline later in the game, maybe I can influence them."

Buffalo Sabres captain Peca also believes that he can make an impact as his team's on-ice advocate when it comes time for the referee to dispense discipline.

"You don't want to challenge them too openly because they might lose respect for you, and then they may not give your team the benefit of the doubt," Peca says.

On the other hand, the captain is expected by teammates to present his case as if he's F. Lee Bailey delivering a passionate summation to the jury.

"There are obviously times you can't keep your cool too much because things are going on that you just don't agree with," Peca says. "But for the most part I've been trying to take a diplomatic approach."

Primeau says referees are far more tolerant of a captain not holding his tongue than they would be of a regular player because refs respect the NHL tradition that demands a captain have his say.

"They understand you are speaking on behalf of all twenty players and the coaching staff," Primeau says. "Whereas when an individual player berates a ref it's for his own personal reasons."

There is no book on how to deal with referees; a captain is often like a lawyer who must learn that different approaches work with different judges.

"There is a different way to approach different refs and use it to your advantage," Primeau says. "But I do know that they frown on you approaching them in a derogatory manner if you aren't wearing a letter (on your sweater)."

Yzerman insists that he does "very little" in his role as captain because the Red Wings have a host of natural leaders. But throughout the league, it's known that the Red Wings feed off Yzerman's intensity. He's hockey's equivalent of the general who leads from the front of the charge instead of from the back. He's the captain zipping across the front with his sabre drawn. Like Messier, Yzerman isn't shy about using his sabre or exploring his dark side in the name of winning, traits that most general managers want in a leader. Yzerman understands the fine line between being a dirty player and being a player who is willing to do whatever it takes to win. Yzerman's reputation is completely different than it was when he was considered only an offensive star.

"I think when Yzerman got the first 'C,' without a doubt he was our best player," says Ken Holland. "But he had to get us points then because if he didn't get them, no one else would. He couldn't spend energy blocking shots. Now we have a better team, and he has changed his game to give us a better chance of winning."

In winning back-to-back Stanley Cups, Yzerman saw what needed to be done, and he did it. That's another aspect of captaincy that isn't written anywhere, but is clearly understood.

EUROPEAN PLAYERS

Toronto Maple Leafs president Ken Dryden compares the European players' situation to what he witnessed when he did a study of foreign children trying to adapt to the Canadian school system. He found that the immigrants did well in their studies, particularly in math. But what was most difficult for them was adjusting socially.

"Math has universal language that they can handle, but they aren't as comfortable (relating to people) in a second language," Dryden says.

European players are at ease on the ice, but it takes time to feel at ease in a dressing room setting in which insults and humor fly around at warp speed. Europeans must earn their stripes as leaders in the room as well as on the ice.

Just imagine a nineteen-year-old American trying to fit into a German computer company with limited German language skills. He might be able to do fantastic work because he understands computer circuitry, but it will be difficult for him to climb the promotions ladder because he can't play politics around the water cooler or participate comfortably in lunchroom banter.

That's why many teenage European hockey players are trying to learn English even before they get drafted. Jagr doesn't believe that the pressure on Europeans to prove themselves is as critical as it was when he signed as an eighteen-year-old in 1990.

"There are so many Europeans in the league," he says. "I think the North Americans and the fans started respecting the European players. When I first came here, I was the first European player for the Penguins and everybody looked at me differently. I couldn't speak English. But in these eight or nine years, it has changed."

Most coaches say it doesn't matter what a player's first language is, providing he can communicate through words or deeds and is willing to do whatever it takes to succeed.

Pittsburgh's Jaromir Jagr and Chicago's Steve Larmer brace for impact as they get closer to the boards.

CHAPTER ELEVEN

The NHL's Most Intense Rivalry

THE DETROIT RED WINGS
AND THE COLORADO AVALANCHE

One indication of emotions boiling beyond the point of no return is when players' mothers start coming up in on-ice conversations. But it might have been when Detroit coach Scotty Bowman put then-Colorado coach Marc Crawford's father's name into play that the Red Wings-Avalanche rivalry reached Def Con 5 status.

During a 1997 playoff game that included 204 penalty minutes in the third period alone, Crawford scaled the glass separating the two benches and screamed wildly at Bowman, associate coach Barry Smith, and Detroit players Kris Draper and Steve Yzerman. According to a *Detroit News* report, Crawford became further unglued when Bowman shouted back: "I knew your father before you did. And I don't think he would be too proud of what you are doing right now."

After the game, Bowman said that Crawford's "eyes were coming out of his head" during his tantrum.

Welcome to the Detroit Red Wings-Colorado Avalanche rivalry, where Bowman frequently practices amateur psychology without a license and good taste gives way to great hockey and the NHL's wildest and most intense rivalry. This is the rivalry with the most passion and grittiness. This is San Francisco 49ers-Green Bay Packers, North Carolina-Duke, and Federation-Borg all rolled into one. This is the type of rivalry in which the aggression and deviousness players show on the ice is matched only by the aggression and deviousness fans show off the ice. This is a rivalry with so much bad blood that Denver fans argue that Red Wings winger Kirk Maltby deserves jail time and Detroit fans believe that Colorado bad boy Claude Lemieux is practically the devil's descendent.

In May of 1999, Denver's KKFN sports talk host Craig Carton asked callers on the air who they would choose if they could "take out" one Red Wings player during the Colorado-Detroit playoff series.

"People have been pretty creative with how they would like to see guys taken out," says Carton. "For a real laid-back, conservative town, you would be shocked at some of the answers you get."

This is a rivalry so nuclear that reportedly a Detroit fan smeared dog doo-doo on Lemieux's car door handle in the name of team spirit. In 1997, an unknown perpetrator, presumed to be a Red Wings fan, kept pulling the fire alarm at a Troy hotel so the Avalanche couldn't get a decent night's sleep during their playoff series.

On the ice, player shenanigans have involved all levels of mayhem, including, and not restricted to, goaltenders squaring off in a fight at center ice, multiple slashes, suspensions, coaches screaming at each other, and some of the most competitive, entertaining hockey the NHL has witnessed in the late 1990s.

"This is just two great hockey teams butting heads," says Red Wings defenseman Mathieu Dandenault. "Our two teams have won the last three Stanley Cups (1995-96, 1996-97, 1997-98). There is a lot of emotion in every game. There is so much hatred between the two teams that even a win in the regular season is an unbelievable feeling."

What makes the rivalry so intriguing is that both teams are full of elite-level talent. The Avalanche won the Stanley Cup in 1996, and the Red Wings won back-to-back titles in 1997 and 1998.

Possibly ten or eleven players on these two teams in 1998-99 could end up in the Hall of Fame. The sure bets include Colorado's Patrick Roy, plus Detroit's Steve Yzerman, Larry Murphy, Chris Chelios, and Igor Larionov (who also made contributions in international hockey). Colorado's Joe Sakic and Peter Forsberg also seem headed that way, and there are other players with a shot.

The vitriol in this rivalry has been burning like a wild brush fire since the 1996 playoff series, when the Avalanche downed Detroit in six games en route to the championship. In 1997, the Red Wings plowed through the Avalanche to win their first championship since 1955. "It's a good story with good plots," says Detroit center Kris Draper.

Only a highly skilled Hollywood screenwriter could come up with a script that matches this rivalry in number of twists and subplots. The Borg vs. Federation comparison works until one must decide which of these teams is the despicable Borg and which is the beloved Federation. Fans in Colorado are sure the Red Wings are a collection of thugs and gangsters, while Detroit fans view Lemieux as the NHL's answer to Darth Maul and Patrick Roy as the patron saint of arrogance.

For three years the two teams have battled with sticks, fists, and words, and there's no indication that the rivalry has run its course. Detroit grinder Kirk Maltby refreshed the hatred in 1998-99 when he fractured Valeri Kamensky's forearm with a slash early in the season.

"It wasn't blatant," Maltby insists. "It was a play that happens every game, and it just happened to get him in the spot where there is no protection."

Avalanche fans saw it differently. "Typically fans (hate) Darren McCarty most," Carton says. "But this year it's focused on Kirk Maltby because he also took a shot (at) Peter Forsberg last game. The hatred is doubled up on Maltby."

Colorado center Peter Forsberg (No. 21) makes $10 million per season because of his offensive ability, but those who watch the game closely will note that he's a rugged competitor who will back down from no one. He plays the game with his elbows elevated. He's extremely strong on his skates and opponents say running into him can be the equivalent of running head first into a stone wall.

Kris Draper is also subject to intense dislike, probably because his close friendship with McCarty is well documented. McCarty became a Detroit hero for life after he bloodied Lemieux in retaliation for Lemieux's hit on Draper, a hit that injured Draper's face so severely that plastic surgery was required. Last year, KKFN gave away tickets to people who called when they heard a crying baby on the air. The baby was supposed to be Draper.

Even the changes the two teams made late in the 1998-99 season seemed like they were designed to help escalate the conflict. The Avalanche added fire hydrant-sized superstar Theo Fleury, an elite-level offensive player who is as fast as a roadrunner and as prickly as a porcupine. He's known as one of the league's most skilled trash talkers. Colorado also added Dale Hunter, who ranks second on the NHL's all-time penalty list. Hunter played for the Washington Capitals last season and he and Detroit captain Steve Yzerman traded slashes and words in last year's Stanley Cup Final. Meanwhile, the Red Wings added Chris Chelios and Ulf Samuelsson, two defensemen whose grating styles of play frequently test the outside boundaries of the rules.

Adding these players to the series is the hockey equivalent of pouring gasoline onto the bonfire.

Fans in Detroit get as riled up about the Avalanche as Colorado fans get about the Red Wings. Two years ago, WDFN radio in Detroit handed out "Screw Lemieux" T-shirts. In 1999, the *Detroit News* conducted a poll to determine the most disliked member of the Avalanche: Lemieux won easily, attaining 64 percent of the 3,100 votes cast. Lemieux, historically a nasty and efficient postseason performer, said he knew just how big the rivalry was when he took a vacation to Hawaii in 1996 and the islander helping him with his bags said matter-of-factly: "You're the bad dude." McCarty vs. Lemieux is always a headline match-up in this series, but the undercard duels can also be R-rated. There are enough villains on these two teams to produce a credible league-wide most-wanted list. "There's always a lot to write about and talk about and show on TV in this series," Lemieux says.

Scotty Bowman, whose head coaching career dates to the 1960s, likens the Colorado-Detroit rivalry to the Montreal-Boston rivalry in the 1970s, or the Montreal-Toronto rivalry before that. It's also been compared to the battle of Alberta in the 1980s, when Edmonton dueled with Calgary en route to their Stanley Cup championships, and the battle of Quebec between the Montreal Canadiens and

Quebec Nordiques. But the Detroit-Colorado rivalry is clearly heightened by the fact that these teams represent two of the top three teams in the league today.

"It's important when we play to respect the rivalry, but not get caught up in the circus," says Detroit winger Brendan Shanahan.

Detroit's WDFN talk show host Mike Stone got fans' juices flowing in 1999 when he asked fans to debate whether Detroit's Sergei Fedorov or Colorado's Peter Forsberg is the better player. "I got hammered because I thought Forsberg was a better player," Stone says, chuckling.

Regardless of who is right, Stone was simply firing the starting gun to mark the beginning of another round of hostilities. In 1999, the Avalanche fell behind 2-0 in the best-of-seven series and then reeled off four consecutive wins to take the series, thereby adding another layer to the rivalry.

"I think this is the best rivalry in professional sports," Stone says. "I don't think anything comes close right now. There are years when Yankees-Red Sox, or Celtics-Sixers, or Pistons-Bulls are big, but for the last few years this has been the best."

ANATOMY OF HATRED

Here's a look at the incidents since 1996 that have added fuel to the Colorado Avalanche-Detroit Red Wings rivalry, considered to be the most intense in the National Hockey League:

In the 1996 playoffs, Detroit's Slava Kozlov pushed Colorado defenseman Adam Foote's face into a seam in the Plexiglas, causing a cut that required twenty stitches to close. Colorado's Claude Lemieux sucker punched Kozlov in Game 3 in retaliation for the Foote incident. In the same 1996 playoff series, then-Colorado coach Marc Crawford took a rip at Detroit coach Scotty Bowman with this quote: "Scotty is a great thinker, but he thinks so much that the plate in his head causes interference in our headsets during the game." Crawford was referring to the steel plate that was affixed to Bowman's skull to help the healing process of a fracture suffered early in his playing career. In Game 6 of the series, Lemieux checked Kris Draper from behind into the boards, causing such severe fractures to Draper's face that plastic surgery was required. Lemieux was suspended for two games in the Stanley Cup Final.

In March of 1997, Detroit's Darren McCarty pummeled Lemieux in retaliation for the hit he laid against Draper the season before. Lemieux was bloodied in the attack. In the same game, Detroit goaltender Mike Vernon and Colorado netminder Patrick Roy squared off in a fight at center ice. The Red Wings say they were unified by the brawl with Colorado. In the 1997 playoffs, Crawford scaled the glass separating the two benches to hurl obscenities at Bowman, Detroit associate coach Barry Smith, and Detroit captain Steve Yzerman. In one 1997 playoff game, Draper took Peter Forsberg out of the game with a "low bridge" hit. Mike Keane removed Detroit's Igor Larionov from the game with a slash to the back of his leg.

The following season, Lemieux dropped his gloves to fight McCarty. Detroit goaltender Chris Osgood and Roy also fought. In the 1998-99 season, Detroit's Kirk Maltby broke Valeri Kamensky's forearm with a slash and was suspended by the league for three games. In Game 1 of the 1999 playoffs, Colorado's Peter Forsberg pushed Brendan Shanahan into the glass, causing Shanahan to need more than forty stitches to close the cut. Forsberg was ejected from the game. In the same game, Darren McCarty received a major penalty for checking Lemieux from behind. After Colorado won the 1999 playoffs, McCarty refused to shake Lemieux's hand, as has been his custom since 1996.

CHAPTER TWELVE

Hockey's Ugliest Moment

THE MAKI-GREEN INCIDENT

More and more, today's defendants are using their upbringing, their environment, or extenuating circumstances to explain a criminal act. They argue that had they been exposed to different influences, variables, and moral codes, they wouldn't have broken the law.

Given how defense strategies have evolved, Wayne Maki's explanation for his violent stick swing against Ted Green was ahead of its time.

The incident happened on September 20, 1969, during an exhibition game between Maki's St. Louis Blues and Green's Boston Bruins in Ottawa. According to testimony in the criminal case six months later, the two players' tussle seemed to begin with Maki holding Green's jersey. Accounts vary on what happened next. Green testified that he shoved Maki and then Maki speared him in the testicles. Hugh Fraser Cameron, a sports reporter, testified that he saw Green give Maki an elbow to the chin, and then saw Maki spear him.

What happened next was very clear to those who witnessed it. Green's stick came down on Maki's shoulder and Maki brought his stick down to strike Green in the head.

"It was scary," remembers former Bruins goaltender Ed Johnston. "His face was all out of whack when he was going down onto the ice."

When Green, considered one of the league's roughest players, slumped to the ice, it was clear he was in trouble. He went into convulsions and was rushed to a nearby hospital, where surgeons immediately performed the first of three operations needed to repair his fractured skull.

"I thought he was gone," Johnston says. "I went into the hospital and stayed there, thinking he might not make it."

A plastic plate was inserted in his head to repair the damage. Green says he didn't even know what happened until a few days after his operation, when he saw a picture of himself and Maki on the cover of a newspaper sticking out of a garbage can.

Because of the level of outrage over the incident, criminal charges were leveled against both Green and Maki, who was twenty-four at the time. The subsequent trials essentially allowed fans a frank look at the NHL's jungle-like mentality, which drove players to believe they had to push the limits of decency to survive. During Maki's trial, it was even brought up that superstar Bobby Orr, the league's most majestic player, had swung his stick at Maki as Maki was being escorted off the ice. According to eyewitness testimony, Orr swung hard enough to break the blade of his stick when it struck the boards.

Green, who twice before had led the NHL in fighting majors, was considered one of the NHL's most feared ruffians, and Maki was simply trying to make the team after being acquired from Chicago in the off-season. In taking on Green, Maki was well out of his league, like a novice competing against a grand master. When it came to roughhousing, Green was an accomplished artist. Had they dropped gloves, Green presumably would have devoured Maki like a lion would feast on a gazelle. But unfortunately for both men, it did not play out that way. In his sworn testimony, St. Louis Blues general manager Lynn Patrick admitted that he thought Maki "was a little foolish" for confronting Green, who was twenty-eight at the time and a nine-year veteran.

Maki saw the situation differently, and his testimony provided a glimpse of how the league's food chain worked. In essence, he said that hockey's unspoken code demanded that he stand up to Green. (An argument could be made that what was true then remains true today: reputations are important to a player, particularly when it comes to physical play.) Maki was trying to prove something to Green, though he certainly didn't intend for it to escalate into a medical emergency.

"I turned to face him because of his reputation," Maki said. "He had already hit me twice, and his stick was up and he made a motion for me."

In a defining moment in the trial, Maki seemed to suggest that in order to play in the NHL, a player had to live by a code that is different from the laws of society. He said that being punched and banged in the face or having a stick near your head "was part of the game."

When crown attorney John Cassells attacked Maki for being too reckless with his stick by anyone's standards, Maki said: "They will run you right out of the league if you skate away from a player like that. It would soon get around that I'm a scaredy-kid. You can't let anyone push you around. It's my career."

Maki also insisted that he was in a defensive posture. "I saw him hit Doug Mohns over the head (the season before). I just swung in desperation to protect myself."

Truthfully, the prevailing sentiment around the league at the time was that law enforcement should stay out of the hockey business. There was much concern that if Maki and Green were convicted, prosecutors would be coming after anyone who participated in a confrontation on the ice. At the time, it was widely believed that players could police the game themselves. If Maki was to be punished, Green or one of his teammates would do it later, which would have happened if Green had not asked them not to do it. In an interview with the *Edmonton Journal* twenty years later, Green said he dictated a letter to his wife, who sent it to the Bruins. "I told them I wasn't looking for revenge; it was nobody's fault. It was allowed in the game then."

At Green's trial, defense attorney Edward Houston also presented a picture of players living in a different world where violence was a way of life. Asked whether it was possible to play hockey without body contact, Green replied that it was. "But you wouldn't keep your job very long."

Driving home the point more succinctly, Green said: "Certainly on (the Bruins) club, I don't think there are too many guys who wear lace panties out there."

Both men eventually were cleared, although in Maki's case, Judge C. Edward Carter put the NHL on notice by saying that sports participation doesn't make players "immune from criminal prosecution." Carter cleared Maki on the grounds that he was defending himself.

Both Maki and Green returned to the NHL—Green one year after the incident. He wore a specially designed helmet, but by all accounts he wasn't the player he once was. Green then went into coaching, and is now an assistant coach for the Edmonton Oilers. Maki was taken by the Vancouver Canucks and played there for three years, until he was diagnosed with a brain tumor. He died on May 13, 1974.

The Green-Maki stick-swinging incident wasn't the first or the last duel in the NHL—just the ugliest. Legend has it that Hall of Famer Sprague Cleghorn was once convicted and fined $50 for clubbing a player. Of course, the great Maurice "Rocket" Richard was suspended for the remainder of the 1955 season, including the playoffs, after smashing his stick over then-Boston defenseman Hal Laycoe, who had high-sticked the Rocket. In the 1970s, Wilf Paiement took a base-ball swing at Detroit's Dennis Polonich's face. This case also ended up in the civil courts, and Polonich was eventually awarded mone-tary damages. Such lawlessness has been moderated in today's game by harsher penalties and common sense. But players around the league still insist that sticks are often carried too high. This has been an area of concern for many years, and the league has aggressively tried to convince players to keep their sticks down; today, even an accidental high stick results in a double minor called against a player. The NHL today says that every player must be responsible for his stick, regardless of whether or not the action was premeditated or inadvertent.

What no one understood in 1969 at the time of the Green-Maki case was that the accompanying criminal case would create an impres-sion about hockey in the United States that would be difficult to change. The brawl-filled 1970s followed, and the sport's national growth was set back another quarter of a century. But as ugly as the Maki-Green incident was, it wasn't the most tragic scene in NHL history. That had occurred a year before in Minnesota, when the NHL experienced its first and last on-ice death.

CHAPTER THIRTEEN

The NHL's
Most Tragic Evening
THE DEATH OF BILL MASTERTON

When Bill Masterton was playing college hockey at the University of Denver in 1960-61, he was as comfortable in a helmet as we are in socks. He wore one in practice. He wore one in games. It was an NCAA rule, and he lived with it without complaint.

During the 1967-68 National Hockey League season, a bareheaded Masterton was abiding by a different rule—an unwritten credo understood by every player in the league.

He lived with that rule without complaint too until it played a role in his death, on January 15, 1968. "The word at that time was that anyone who wore a helmet was liable not to have a job," says Ted Hampson, who was playing for the Oakland Seals that fateful night. "It was unstated. It was just a way of hockey. I think that's why Bill Masterton didn't wear a helmet. It was undoubtedly hinted that he shouldn't wear one."

Masterton had retired from the Montreal Canadiens' farm system in 1963, convinced that the odds were against him in advancing to the show in such a talent-laden organization. Masterton was a smart, playmaking forward who had dominated offensively in college. Almost forty years after graduating, his production of 2.2 points per game still shines as the Denver record. In 3 years of eligibility, Masterton had 66 goals and 130 assists in 89 games. On the ice, he frequently looked like a creative craftsman among common laborers. His plays were memorable, and they were essential to Denver's winning of back-to-back NCAA titles in 1960 and 1961.

With seventeen goals and twenty-seven assists in twenty-two games, Masterton won the Western Collegiate Hockey Association scoring title in 1959-60. But his best season may have been 1960-61, when he led Denver to a 30-1-1 record.

"He was a dominant player in college," says his former Denver roommate Marshall Johnston, now the Ottawa Senators' general manager.

But college players weren't readily accepted in the NHL at that time. Gordon "Red" Berenson had stepped directly from the University of Michigan to the NHL in 1961-62, but it hadn't created a rush to sign college players. NHL general managers had no love for ex-college players, and Masterton's presence simply made him an exception to the rule. Even if he had thought about wearing a helmet, he probably wouldn't have under those circumstances (even though Berenson had kept his on).

Helmet wearers were viewed as lightweights in a world in which a man's reputation was almost as important to him as his skating ability.

"He wasn't a great skater, but he had great hands. He wasn't a power forward, but physical play didn't bother him, either," says Johnston, who kept his helmet on when he turned pro after leaving Denver, but can speculate why Masterton might have taken his off. "You weren't considered macho if you wore one," Johnston recalls.

He compares this past reluctance to wear a helmet to today's reluctance to wear a half visor, although many are wearing them. "Ray Bourque has put a mask on, but twenty years ago if he would have put a mask on it might have been a different story," Johnston

Hall of Fame defenseman Tim Horton slows down Montreal's John Ferguson, whose contributions went beyond his punching ability. He received so much room on the ice that he was also able to make significant offensive contributions.

(Photo courtesy of John Ferguson)

says. "In fact, twenty years ago I don't think he would have put one on."

One of the jokes of the era was that a reporter once asked an NHL superstar why he did not wear a helmet to protect his brain, though he wore a cup and a jock to protect his genitals.

"Because," said the star, "I can always pay someone to do my thinking for me."

Former NHL defenseman Bob Plager remembers the intense peer pressure in those days to play without a helmet. "In those days, if you wore one, you were the sissy," he remembers.

Also working against Masterton at the NHL level was his lack of pure speed. That may have helped convince him to leave the Canadiens when he was twenty-four. Upon retirement, he returned to Denver, earned a master's degree, and then accepted a job in contract administration with Honeywell in Minneapolis. He was working there when the Minnesota North Stars were granted an NHL franchise. It was Minnesota coach Wren Blair who talked Masterton into revisiting his dream of playing in the NHL.

Returning to the game worked out well for Masterton, who was considered one of Minnesota's most trustworthy players. He compensated for his lack of speed by becoming a dependable two-way player. The twenty-nine-year-old center boasted four goals and seven assists heading toward the All-Star break in January, and the North Stars were pleased with his production. When Masterton stepped onto the ice to play against the Oakland Seals on January 13, 1968, there was no reason to think anything but that he had made the right decision to return to the sport he loved.

All of that changed near the end of the first period when Masterton was sandwiched on hits by Oakland's Ron Harris and Larry Cahan. He was smacked just as he released the puck about twenty

Chicago Blackhawks center Stan Mikita wore a helmet before it was fashionable in the National Hockey League.

to thirty feet in front of the Oakland net. It wasn't a dirty hit, just a big-time wallop—the kind of check that occurred many times before and has occurred many times since. Hampson was on the ice at the time, and saw the play develop. "When he got hit, he was already dazed," Hampson says. "He didn't seem to have any sense of balance. He slammed his head on the ice. Those of us on the ice knew he was in very serious trouble."

Other eyewitnesses also sensed that Masterton was in trouble even before he hit his head. Blair was quoted in newspaper accounts at the time as saying he believed Masterton "was unconscious before he hit the ice."

"I've never seen anybody go down that way," Blair told the *Associated Press*.

Bleeding heavily, Masterton began convulsing immediately. Eyewitnesses reported that he turned blue and was having difficulty breathing. Oakland player Charlie Burns, reacting quickly in a crisis, heroically used his stick to pry open Masterton's mouth to prevent him from swallowing his tongue. But swift medical attention did not save Masterton. Nothing done on the ice could have saved him. Once transported to the hospital, it was determined that he had suffered a massive brain injury. Surgery wasn't even an option. A respirator kept him alive for thirty hours before he died in the early morning hours of January 15.

Masterton's death was the first in the history of the NHL, and it forced the league to confront the issue of whether helmet use should become mandatory. Would he still be alive had he been wearing a helmet? That's what many players were asking themselves the next morning, even if they didn't say much about it publicly. At that point in NHL history, few NHL players were wearing helmets. Andre Boudrias was the only Minnesota player who wore a helmet. Players always complained that they were uncomfortable, too cumbersome, and made their heads sweat too much during the game. Unsaid was that players who wore helmets were considered too delicate for such a manly game.

Players began to talk openly about helmet use, and Toronto Maple Leafs forward Brian Conacher made a statement when he became the first NHL player to wear a helmet in the annual All-Star game. Chicago defenseman Pierre Pilote stunned teammates and fans when he showed up in the next game wearing a helmet after thirteen seasons of playing without one. The Scooter Line of Stan Mikita, Ken Wharram, and Doug Mohns also donned what some called "brain buckets."

Montreal Canadien J. C. Tremblay, one of the few big-time players who was already wearing a helmet before the Masterton tragedy, told the *Toronto Star* he didn't understand those who claimed that a helmet affected how they performed on the ice.

"If I play a bad game, it is me, not my sideburns or helmet," Tremblay said. "Sure I perspire and have to wipe out my eyes once in a while. But that's a small matter."

Even Chicago Blackhawks star Bobby Hull talked about wearing a helmet, although he never followed through with it.

"It is unfortunate that it takes something like this to start you thinking about helmets," he told the media in 1968. "We wear twenty-five pounds of protective equipment on other parts of our bodies and leave the most vulnerable spot unprotected."

Masterton's death, as senseless as it was, did change the game, although it was more of an evolution than an overnight transformation. Even today, the NHL clings to traditions as if Moses brought them down himself. Upon Masterton's death, NHL power brokers were far too stubborn to push for the immediate introduction of mandatory helmets.

Washington's Rod Langway played without a helmet long after everyone had embraced the idea that a helmet was as necessary in hockey as it was in football.

The majority of players had an outwardly stoic reaction to Masterton's death. A rumor started that Masterton might have suffered some level of head injury a week before the incident that could have contributed to his death. Nobody wanted to believe that a clean, everyday check that happens twenty times a game could snuff out Masterton's life. But some around the league clearly were thinking: "That could have been me out there." Slowly, momentum was building to change the helmet rule.

The Ted Green-Wayne Maki stick swinging incident also added some impetus for change. Although no one will say so publicly, an argument can be made that Green's head injury brought even more attention to the helmet issue than Masterton's death, because Green was a more notable player in that era. Green was a rough customer, and when he was sent crumbling to the ice in a heap it certainly dismissed all notions of invincibility.

Helmet use increased in the 1970s, particularly with more college players joining the pro ranks. Behind closed doors, debate over the mandatory use of helmets raged in the league. Traditionalists argued that if the helmets went on, the sticks would come up. That argument dated back to the 1930s, when general manager Art Ross forced members of the Boston Bruins to wear helmets for the remainder of the season after Ace Bailey suffered a career-ending concussion when he was tripped from behind by Eddie Shore. George Boucher, an NHL coach at the time, railed on helmets, saying that helmeted players didn't respect each other and that their sticks would be at eye level in no time.

It wasn't until 1979 that the NHL finally adopted a rule for mandatory helmet use for players who entered the league from that point on. All veteran players who weren't wearing helmets were grandfathered into the rule as exempt. That meant that the last helmetless player wasn't out of the NHL until Craig MacTavish retired after the 1996-97 season.

In 1992-93, then-NHL president Gil Stein, responding to complaints that helmeted players had lost their identity with fans and that sticks were up too high, pushed through a rule that allowed players to sign a waiver to play without a helmet. Six players signed the waiver, but only Calgary's Greg Smyth actually tried it in the preseason. He was wearing one again at the start of the season.

Thirty years after Masterton's death there are new debates about protective equipment. Some now are arguing that the use of protective facial coverage at the youth and college levels has produced a generation of players who feel invincible and take too many chances when they play. NHL scouts claim the college game is dirtier because players wear masks and hence aren't afraid to wield sticks like they're weapons.

Meanwhile, Masterton's memory lives on through a league trophy named after him. A few months after his death, the NHL introduced the Masterton Trophy, to be awarded each year to the player "who best exemplifies the qualities of perseverance, sportsmanship, and dedication to hockey." Ironically, Hampson, who was on the ice when Masterton died, won the Masterton Trophy in 1969.

"The league named the award after Bill Masterton because he died, but it was appropriate," Johnston says. "That's the kind of person he was—he was as classy of a person as you would ever find. He was a modest and quiet leader."

The trophy has evolved into an honor for players who battle back from serious injury and illness to continue their careers. But Masterton's legacy extends beyond his namesake trophy. His death is often mentioned today by those who lobby for changes to make the game safer. In recent years, there has been a growing movement in the NHL to make sure players wear the most protective, certified helmet available because of increasing problems with post-concussion syndrome. There is also a smaller lobby to coax players to wear half-shield visors for added protection. The cry from the pro-shield advocates is that the league must act now before someone suffers blindness or worse from a shot taken to the eyes or forehead. Others are worried that helmets aren't enough to protect players when they smash into the new seamless Plexiglas that seems less forgiving than the glass of old.

Any argument about the need for increased protective equipment can be summed up simply: the league must always remember what happened to Bill Masterton. That is his legacy.

Epilogue
HOCKEY IN THE TWENTY-FIRST CENTURY

"As long as I'm director of hockey operations,
hockey will never turn into ballroom dancing."
—Brian Burke, NHL senior vice president
and director of hockey operations, 1997

To appreciate the role that toughness plays in hockey history, consider that in his pre-NHL days, probably in 1916, future Hall of Famer Sprague Cleghorn was hauled before a local magistrate to face criminal charges for allegedly assaulting a player during a hockey game.

According to folklore, Cleghorn was acquitted on all charges because the victim of the attack, Newsy Lalonde, came in and testified on Cleghorn's behalf. Lalonde, a future Hall of Famer and NHL scoring champion, insisted Cleghorn "was just doing his job."

Hockey's most frustrating dilemma is that the physical attributes that make the sport so attractive to some fans also make it distasteful to others. As the NHL tries to position itself to enjoy a higher national profile in the twenty-first century, the league is clearly in the midst of a period of a self-evaluation. The question posed again and again is how can the NHL change its excessively violent image without losing the energy and crowd appeal that come from the intense contact? "Really, we all want to see more hitting, not less," says Nashville Predators general manager David Poile.

Pittsburgh Penguins' Duane Rupp (No. 2) shows here that NHL defensemen weren't shy about laying the lumber on opponents in the 1970s. That's Detroit's Bruce MacGregor getting chopped while goaltender Al Smith makes the save.

The league clearly doesn't want hockey to become ballet on ice or ballroom dancing. Nobody wants players tiptoeing around the ice, behaving timidly about throwing body checks. What league officials want is for players to stop using their sticks as weapons, or checking from behind, or kicking the skates out from under an opponent, or elbowing an adversary in the head. Even the league's toughest customers will admit that occasionally the violence has been excessive in recent years.

Before the 1998-99 season, the NHL informed teams that it was "raising the bar" with regard to using unpaid suspensions to deter players from using excessive violence. In the first six weeks of the season, Director of Hockey Operations Colin Campbell dealt out six-

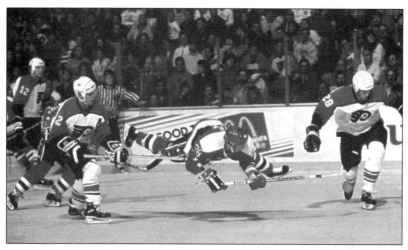

A Washington Capitals player trying to split the Philadelphia defense quickly found himself airborne in a scissor-split.

teen suspensions for a total of fifty-seven games. Los Angeles Kings forward Matt Johnson received a twelve-game suspension for sucker punching New York Rangers defenseman Jeff Beukeboom. Johnson lost more than $90,000 in salary.

"I don't want to hear that players don't respect one another any more," says Campbell, a former NHL player and coach.

Campbell clearly doesn't have much sympathy for the always-popular retaliation defense. "There are certain vehicles in place to retaliate," he says. "You can hit guys—it's a physical game. We like the physical part of the game, but not the craziness of it . . ." While many applauded the league's tougher posture on excessive violence, there were some—even some of the victims—who viewed the crackdown as being too harsh.

"I think sometimes they're being a little too severe," says Colorado's Cam Russell, the victim of a hit that earned Tampa Bay's Andrei Nazarov a seven-game suspension. "Some things are just five-minute penalties, and that's the way it should be. Sometimes it's just a five-minute elbowing penalty. I don't think it should result in a three-game suspension. But that's just the way the league is, and in the long run it will probably help the league."

Nothing stirs passions in hockey more than the debate about fighting. In the 1970s, when a reporter asked then-Minnesota Fighting Saints general manager Glen Sonmor about excessive fighting in the sport, he reportedly said, "If we don't do something about all this fighting we are going to have to build bigger arenas." Nonbelievers often point to the sport's tolerance of fighting as the reason why hockey hasn't gained a stronger foothold in the United States. The league has never been able to overcome the distorted image that hockey has received as a result of the brawl-filled 1970s, the movie *Slap Shot,* and even the old joke about the comedian who went to "a fight and a hockey game broke out." The fact that many sportscasters seem to show fight highlights as much as goal highlights also doesn't help the sport's image.

What those concerns don't address is that some people believe fighting is risky behavior, since a TKO'd fighter lands on ice and not on a canvas. Toronto winger Nick Kypreos's career ended in 1997-98 because of a concussion he suffered when his head hit the ice in a fight with the New York Rangers' Ryan VandenBussche.

"It's not the punch, but the danger of falling six feet out of control that is the problem," says Toronto Maple Leafs president Ken Dryden. The proponents of fighting say enforcers help maintain law and order on the ice. They insist that many players behave themselves out of fear that if they don't they will have to answer to Bob Probert, Tie Domi, or Tony Twist. They insist that fighting is a good release for players who are constantly getting hit in a game. Dryden got nowhere in 1997-98 when he made a plea to fellow general man-

Montreal's Eric Desjardins gets his stick up high against Buffalo's Christian Ruutuu in the late 1980s.

agers to have fighting legislated out of the game. He favors expulsion for a fighter, not a five-minute penalty.

Proponents insist that the league's marquee offensive players might as well have targets on their backs if fighting is legislated out of the game. They argue that all that protects superstars from daily abuse in the NHL are the tough guys who are, in essence, highly paid and respected security guards, entrusted with safeguarding the league's ruling elite. That role is so respected that some of the league's superstars, including Anaheim's Paul Kariya, have called for the abolishment of the instigator rule to give tough guys more freedom to mete out frontier justice.

In its defense, proponents insist that fighting is a good emotional release for players who are constantly getting hit in a game. They also argue that stick work will become more prevalent if fighting is eliminated and that checking from behind and boarding will replace fighting as a means for retaliation. According to fighting proponents, a player is far less likely to get hurt fighting than he would be if he is slashed or flung against the boards when he is vulnerable. They believe that if fighting is removed from the game, some players will be injected with a false sense of bravery, and won't be afraid to slash the superstar because the "protectors" have their hands tied.

The pro-fighter's argument is much like the environmentalist's argument that taking the wolf out of the woods or the spider out of your yard would disrupt the ecosystem. Proponents argue that the wolf, spider, and tough guy all rid the world of creatures far more hideous than they are.

Commissioner Gary Bettman believes the fighting issue isn't as big as some in the media want to make it. "Historically, fighting has been an accepted part of the game," he says. "There are reasons why it has been accepted. One is if you do not have fighting, you will

At 6-foot-5, 230 pounds, Los Angeles Kings youngster Matt Johnson (left), shown here battling Patrick Cote, is quickly developing a reputation as one of the league's truly scary fighters. He has the potential to hurt an opponent if he connects with full force. His punches are nuclear. He's still young, and sometimes out of control. New York Rangers' Jeff Beukeboom said that when Johnson sucker-punched him in a game in 1998-99, Johnson earned a league-imposed twelve-game suspension.

end up with the type of stick work you see in Europe." In Europe, players seem more willing to play with their sticks high because they have no fear of having to defend their actions in a bout against a protector. Players in Europe protect themselves with a slash back.

Brian Burke, who was the league's discipline guru before becoming the Vancouver Canucks' general manager in 1998-99, doesn't believe fighting will be removed from hockey any time in the near future. He says the sport's fans view it as a necessary part of the game. "Nobody in the arena turns his or her back when there's a fight," he says.

There's no denying that a hockey fight puts a charge into an arena, and that fighters are generally among the most popular players on their teams. In the Nashville Predators' first season in the NHL

Goaltenders aren't exempt from physical contact, even though the NHL rules are designed to protect them. Most aren't timid about protecting the space. Here, New York Rangers' Ed Giacomin punches Garry Howatt during one heated game with the New York Islanders in the 1970s.

in 1998-99, it was clear that their nouveau fans enjoyed the toe-to-toe confrontations. Patrick Cote, who led the NHL in fighting majors, was among the team's most popular players. When the Predators were raising money for charity, they auctioned off Cote memorabilia because it brought in the most money. One of his sticks sold for five hundred dollars. The Predators couldn't even get that kind of donation for items from some of the league's most gifted offensive players, like Teemu Selanne or Pierre Turgeon. Cote explains his connection with southern crowds this way: "They may not understand hockey, but they understand fighting."

Cote's popularity notwithstanding, opponents of fighting strongly believe that the presence of fighting at the NHL level stunts its growth. The anti-fighting bloc argues that a large number of sports fans pass up hockey as pro wrestling on skates, and that television ratings for hockey in the United States are weak because U.S. viewers don't take hockey seriously due to its tolerance of fighting.

Fighting has outlived its usefulness as a deterrent, say members of the anti-fighting brigade. With a second referee now patrolling the ice during NHL games, superstars are as well protected as they were by tough guys, particularly now that the NHL is handing out stiffer suspensions to those who use excessive violence. Evidence supports the notion that using two referees discourages fights; in 1998-99, when the NHL was experimenting with both two- and one-referee games, fighting was down about fifteen percent in games in which two referees were present. Anti-fighting lobbyists point out that almost all fighting has been eliminated in the playoffs because the stakes are too high to risk instigator penalties, and yet no one seems to miss fighting in the postseason. People aren't boycotting playoff games just because some of their favorite heavyweights no longer have roles. Blues fans idolize noted pugilists Tony Twist and Kelly Chase during

Ken Klee (Washington) adds some intimidation to his successful take out against Derek Plante.

the regular season, but they didn't take up picket signs when Twist and Chase were used sparingly by coach Joel Quenneville during the 1999 playoffs.

Those who support the idea of having an automatic ejection for fighting also point out that some of the best hockey the world has ever seen has been played at the Canada Cup, the World Cup, and the Olympics, in which fighting is next to nonexistent. Olympic hockey is watched by more people around the world than any other form of hockey, and no one turns off the TV just because there's no fighting.

One theory is that fighting will be eradicated by natural evolution. In 1998-99, the Ottawa Senators earned only a handful of fighting majors all season and finished second in the Eastern Conference. Teams that played the Senators often didn't dress their tough guys because there was no one on the Senators' roster for them to fight. That plan worked well for the Senators all season. But in the first round of the playoffs, the Sabres used their biggest, toughest lineup and punished the Senators physically at every turn. Ottawa superstar Alexei Yashin and his linemates were manhandled by the line of Mike Peca, Vaclav Varada, and Dixon Ward.

After the upset, the prevailing wisdom in the hockey world was that the Senators were pushed around because they had no policeman—no one willing to stand up to the bullies. Theoretically, they should have made the Sabres pay on the power play; but in the playoffs, even with two referees on the ice, more rough play seems to be tolerated. If the Senators would have had more toughness up front, more guys willing to stand up to the Sabres, would Buffalo's Peca have changed his approach? "It wouldn't have changed a thing we did," Peca says. "But it probably would have made (Yashin) more confident to give it back a little bit. But having said that, maybe the one player should be stronger and battle through that."

Working against natural evolutionary change is the fear many general managers have about giving up their tough guys. No one trusts the other general managers to surrender theirs. "It was like the nuclear arms race," Campbell says. "OK, who is going to get rid of theirs first?"

The arguments go on and on without any hint of a resolution in the near future. The expectation is that no anti-fighting legislation will come to the NHL any time soon. However, Dryden believes there will be a time when the anti-fighting forces will carry the day. "Something will happen to refocus it," he says.

The pro-hockey camp certainly hopes that it isn't a life-threatening injury that causes the refocus on fighting's place in hockey. They know that everyone is thrilled to watch the tightrope walker—until he drops off the wire. Then, everyone wants to know who the hell let him up there.